THE THIRD FREEDOM

ENDING HUNGER IN OUR TIME

GEORGE McGOVERN

Simon & Schuster

New York   London   Toronto   Sydney   Singapore

SIMON & SCHUSTER
Rockefeller Center
1230 Avenue of the Americas
New York, NY 10020

Book design by Ellen R. Sasahara

Manufactured in the United States of America

1   3   5   7   9   10   8   6   4   2

Library of Congress Cataloging-in-Publication Data
McGovern, George S. (George Stanley), 1922–
    The third freedom : ending hunger in our time / George McGovern.
    p. cm.
Includes index
    1. Food relief—Political aspects. 2. Food relief—International coopera-
tion. 3. Hunger—Prevention. 4. Food relief, America—Economic aspects.
I. Title.

HV696.F6 M394 2001
363.8—dc21   00-049231
                    ISBN 0-684-85334-5

For Pat Donovan—
my matchless secretary of many years

CONTENTS

IN THE FUTURE DAYS, WHICH WE SEEK to make secure, we look forward to a world founded upon four essential human freedoms.

The first is freedom of speech and expression—everywhere in the world.

The second is freedom of every person to worship God in his own way—everywhere in the world.

The third is freedom from want—which, translated into world terms, mean economic understanding which will secure to every nation a healthy peacetime life for its inhabitants—everywhere in the world.

The fourth is freedom from fear—which, translated into world terms, means a worldwide reduction of armaments to such a point and in such a thorough fashion that no nation will be in a position to commit an act of physical aggression against any neighbor—anywhere in the world.

—FRANKLIN D. ROOSEVELT, from his 1941
State of the Union address

PREFACE

HUNGER IS A POLITICAL CONDITION. The earth has enough knowledge and resources to eradicate this ancient scourge. Hunger has plagued the world for thousands of years. But ending it is a greater moral imperative now than ever before, because for the first time humanity has the instruments in hand to defeat this cruel enemy at a very reasonable cost. We have the ability to provide food for all within the next three decades. Consider just one encouraging statistic: When I ran for the presidency in 1972, 35 percent of the world's people were hungry. By 1996, while the global population had expanded, only 17 percent of the earth's people were hungry—half the percentage of three decades ago. This is an impressive fact, particularly in view of the gloomy prophecies of the 1960s that population growth was racing ahead of food production. Widespread famines across the Third World were also predicted. Clearly the gains in food production from scientific farming, including the Green Revolution, plus the slowing of population growth have reduced hunger in the developing countries.

Here are some other encouraging statistics: The world now produces a quantity of grain that, if distributed evenly, would provide everyone with 3,500 calories per day, more than enough for an optimal diet. This does not even count vegetables, fruits, fish, meat, poultry, edible oils, nuts, root crops, or dairy products. Despite the dire predictions that the world's population would soon outstrip food production, it has been the other way around: food production has risen a full 16 percent above population growth.

The American Association for the Advancement of Science has noted that 78 percent of the world's malnourished children live in countries with food surpluses. Clearly, this condition indicates a need for a keener social conscience and better political leadership.

A 1996 United Nations survey that is regarded as the most accurate forecast available estimated that world population will peak and then level off near the year 2050 at just under 10 billion—an increase of 4 billion over the present total. Population may then decline somewhat, because of lower birthrates. Such predictions are uncertain. It may be that advances in medicine and health care will enable people to live longer, thus offsetting declining birth rates. Although a population of 10 billion will tax some resources, projected increases in food production indicate that the world can feed that many people a half-century from now. As we will see from the pages that follow, the nations and peoples of the world will have to take a series of common-sense steps to ensure that everyone is fed. But there is no need for panic or scare tactics. There is enough food to go around now and for at least the next half-century. The world is not going to run out of food for all. Those readers young enough now to be around in the year 2050 will need to consider other measures that will take the world safely through the last half of the century, to 2100. But who can even guess what scientific gains will come into the hands and minds of future generations?

Having grappled for years with the global hunger challenge and the American domestic condition, I am sure that we have the resources and the knowledge to end hunger everywhere. The big question is, Do we have the political leadership and the will to end this scourge in our time?

One of my admired friends of long standing was the late Archbishop Dom Helder Camara of Brazil. He once observed: "When I give food to the poor, they call me a saint. When I ask why the poor have no food, they call me a communist." I learned much about the burdens and hurts of the poor from this good man. Following his example, I have tried in this book to ask the hard questions and then to seek the sometimes difficult answers.

I am deeply gratified that the United Nations food and agriculture agencies in Rome, to which I am now the American ambassador, are committed to reducing the number of hungry people in the world by half by the year 2015. That goal is within the reach of the international community. We should be willing and able by the year 2030 to end hunger for the remaining 400 million chronically hungry inhabitants of our planet.

Two questions need to be considered together in a treatise about world hunger: (1) What would it cost for the nations of the world, acting through the United Nations, to end hunger? and (2) What will be the cost if we permit hunger to continue at its present level? Of the scores of experts with the UN agencies in Rome chiefly involved in the global hunger issue, I have yet to meet a single one—conservative, liberal, or mugwump—who doesn't believe that the cost to the world of hunger is vastly greater than the cost of ending it. I can think of no investment that would profit the international community more than erasing hunger from the face of the earth.

So what will it cost? Beyond what the United States and other countries are now doing, it will take an estimated $5 billion a year, of which $1.2 billion would come from the United States. If this annual allocation were continued for fifteen years, until 2015, we could reduce the 800 million hungry people by half. To erase hunger for the remaining 400 million would cost about the same if it were to be accomplished in the 15 years leading up to the year 2030.

The U.S. Agency for International Development puts the cost at $2.6 billion annually, whereas the UN Food and Agriculture Organization estimates the cost higher at $6 billion. My figure of $5 billion annually—which is based on my own judgment of the cost of some of the steps I would like to see taken, including especially a universal school lunch program for every child in the world—is $2.4 billion higher than USAID's but still a billion below the United Nations figure. I concur with the estimate of the respected Bread for the World Institute in Silver Spring, Maryland, that it would take another $5 billion—largely in updating our food stamp program—to meet the needs of the 31 million inadequately fed Americans. Thus, the total American cost internationally and domestically would be an additional $6.2 billion a year—a fraction of what we now spend on cigarettes, beer, or cosmetics. If we decided to enact a modest increase in the minimum wage, we could cut the increase in food stamps in half.

What will it cost if we *don't* end the hunger that now afflicts so many of our fellow humans? The World Bank has concluded that each year malnutrition causes the loss of 46 million years of productive life, at a cost of $16 billion annually, several times the cost of ending hunger and turning this loss into productive gain.

Of course it is impossible to evaluate with dollars the real cost of hunger. What is the value of a human life? The twentieth century was the most violent in human history, with nearly 150 million people killed by war. But in just the last half of that century nearly three times as many died of malnutrition or related causes. How does one put a dollar figure on this terrible toll silently collected by the Grim Reaper? What is the cost of 800 million hungry people dragging through shortened and miserable lives, unable to study, work, play, or otherwise function normally because of the ever-present drain of hunger and malnutrition on body, mind, and spirit? What is the cost of millions of young mothers breaking under the despair of watching their children waste away and die from malnutrition? This is a problem we can resolve at a fraction of the cost of ignoring it. We need to be about that task now. I give you my word that anyone who looks honestly at world hunger and measures the cost of ending it for all time will conclude that this is a bargain well worth seizing. More often than not, those who look at the problem and the cost of its solution will wonder why humanity didn't resolve it long ago.

As an American I have always thought that I live in the greatest country on earth. If we will now take the lead in ending world hunger, as only we can do, we will be an even greater country, and God's blessing and that of our fellow humans will be upon us.

But victory over hunger will not come without the assistance of those countries able to help, including the European nations, Japan, Canada, Australia, Argentina, and the OPEC oil states. And before the battle is over, perhaps it can be joined by China, India, and Russia. Of equal or greater importance is the need for reform in the developing countries if hunger is to be ended. This means improved farming methods; the conservation and wiser use of the earth's limited water resources; more rights and opportunities—especially education—for the girls and women of the Third

World; a greater measure of democratic government responsive to basic human needs, including food security; and a substitution of commonsense negotiation of differences instead of the murderous civil, ethnic, and nationalistic conflicts that have torn up people, property, and land across the Third World. It is estimated that 10 percent of the world's hungry people are in that condition because of the disruptions of war and other civil strife. People in villages and on farms, including poor women and men, as well as city dwellers, need to be involved in political and economic decisions that affect their lives. Education and democracy may be the most powerful combatants in the war on hunger and poverty.

These are a few of the conditions that need to be confronted to build for the first time the architecture of food security on our planet.

My own experience with these issues probably began when I was a boy growing up on the agricultural and ranching plains of South Dakota. Later on, when I was at about the midpoint of my twenty-two-year career in the House and Senate of the United States, the *New York Times* ran a feature article that read, in part: "Food, farmers and his fellow man—those are the foundation stones upon which George McGovern has built his philosophy of life." I treasure that article because it does indeed describe the interests and principles that have guided much of my public career.

In South Dakota, I saw some of the world's best farmers floundering because they could not sell their surplus production for a break-even price. At the same time I read of hunger and starvation in other parts of the world. That cruel paradox bothered me in the 1930s as a teenager; it still does in the year 2000.

Preface

In the 1960s President John Kennedy gave me a wonderful opportunity to deal directly with the challenge of farm surpluses in a world of hungry people. For two years prior to entering the U.S. Senate, I served in the Executive Office of the President as director of the newly created office of Food for Peace. Those two years became one of the most satisfying experiences of my life, opening up to me the vast vistas of world hunger and giving me a chance to test in the field some of the most promising solutions.

Now, nearly forty years later, with my House and Senate years and a heart-stirring, head-filling campaign for the presidency behind me, I find myself again in Rome, the Eternal City. I first came here in 1944 as a twenty-two-year-old bomber pilot. At that time Italy was suffering from the ravages of war and a destructive leadership that left millions of people in dire need and acute hunger. Today, I am surrounded by some of the world's finest restaurants and food markets. The Italian people may be the world's best fed. I'm keenly aware of the dramatic contrast between the bountiful gourmet foods of Rome and the all-too-meager diets of so much of the world around us.

I'm grateful to have survived thirty-five bombing missions over Nazi Germany and to be back in Italy so many years later—still serving my government, but this time as one who is distributing food rather than bombs.

Working here in Rome and traveling out from time to time to meet the hungry, poor, and sick around the globe, I recall a Scripture first read to me in childhood by my father: "The Spirit of the Lord is upon me, because he hath anointed me to preach the gospel to the poor; he hath sent me to heal the broken-hearted, to preach deliverance to the captives, and recovering of sight to the blind, to set at liberty them that are bruised" (Luke 4:18). I can't live up to all the lofty implications of this testimony from Luke, but I'm grateful to President Bill Clinton and the American people for giving me an opportunity to do the best I can. This book is part of that effort. I pray that in God's good time it may bring some measure of healing to the poor, the bruised, and the broken-hearted of the earth.

CHAPTER 1

A STRATEGY TO DEFEAT
WORLD HUNGER

IN THE BLISTERING, heart-rending drought and depression days of 1932 I was a ten-year-old boy growing up in Mitchell, South Dakota. Most of the time I was a contented youngster, but some memories are not pleasant. A lifetime later, I recall the huge boiling dust clouds that rolled across the parched Dakota plains, hiding the sun in a darkness like midnight. The finely ground dirt not only blackened the sky; it came hard at the crevices of our eyes, ears, noses, and throats. The tiniest cracks or openings in windows and doors ushered the dust inside.

The first such fearful storm that I remember happened during a summer hike several miles east of Mitchell with my boyhood friend Vernon Hersey. After failing efforts to grope our way in the blinding dust to a country road, Vernon suggested that the Milwaukee railroad tracks would lead us back to Mitchell. We followed them homeward, listening over the howling wind for a train whistle.

When the Dakota sun was not blotted out by dust storms, it was frequently shrouded by flying grasshopper invasions. They could strip growing crops down to the ground in a matter of hours. Farmers who had invested their cash and months of labor in planting and nurturing crops would watch their harvest disappear. The voracious pests would even devour the wooden handles of hoes and pitchforks.

My father was a Wesleyan Methodist clergyman who believed in God, John Wesley (the founder of Methodism), and the St. Louis Cardinals. This "Holy Trinity" helped our household get through the Depression. I knew about the Twelve Apostles, but I knew even more about the Cardinals' "Gashouse Gang"—Dizzy and Daffy Dean, Leo Durocher, Pepper Martin, Joe Medwick, Frankie Frisch—and from that day to this, the first item I have looked for in the morning paper is the standing of the St. Louis Cardinals. (As I write, they are in first place in their division, of course!)

One day in the autumn of 1932, my dad took me pheasant hunting, which included a stop at our friend Art Kendall's farm, ten miles southwest of Mitchell. Kendall was one of my heroes, a hardworking farmer and a devout member of my dad's congregation. I admired his prowess in hunting pheasants, which was not only an enjoyable sport, but also enriched our tables. Art was the best shot with a 12-gauge, double-barreled shotgun I ever saw. He also had a sense of humor—of a kind. On my first trip carrying a small-gauge shotgun, he told me that there was a rabbit just ahead of me. I saw something move and promptly filled it with buckshot. It was a skunk, as Art knew, and it sprayed its dreadful perfume all over me before expiring. I was invited to ride on the outside fender of the car for the rest of the day. I can still hear Art Kendall's laughter.

Not only did I learn about skunks that day, but I received another, more serious lesson. When my dad and I arrived at Art's farm to pick him up, we found him sitting on his back porch looking at a slip of paper. As we approached him, I realized that he had been crying. How could this be—big, strong, brave Art Kendall crying? It was the first time I had seen an adult cry, except for my mother the night Grandma died. Why was he crying? Because he had just received a check for all of his hogs barely big enough to cover the trucker's fee for hauling them to the livestock market in Sioux City, Iowa. Art had worked for a year feeding his corn crop to those hogs and getting them ready for market. In the end, he netted nothing. This was the kind of ruinous price level that choked a farmer's spirit and sent him into bankruptcy.

Over the years, when I saw how hard farmers worked and how little they frequently received for their labor, it broke my heart. That happened for a long, hard decade when I was a boy. A similar downturn has hit the farm economy during the present decade.

In the mid to late 1920s, American farmers were primed to produce. They had geared up a magnificent agricultural machine in response to the demand generated by World War I. Farmers were similarly primed to produce in the mid-1990s. Global demand for American agricultural products was high, and projected to grow higher.

Farmers in the post–World War I period saw the bottom fall out of their markets when foreign countries cinched their belts as war debts forced them to economize. Similarly, the growth projected for agricultural markets in the 1990s has been stunted by the Asian financial crisis. To compound the difficulties, both the mid-1920s and the late 1990s were characterized by larger than average crops—a blessing turned into a curse. Farmers were not earning enough from the sale of their crops or animals to cover production costs in either of these two periods.

Financial stress, then as now, accelerated the trend toward reducing the number of farmers—a trend that technological advances have amplified throughout the century as more food is produced with fewer farmers.

When Henry Wallace became secretary of agriculture in 1933, he put his keen mind to work on crafting the most innovative package of government farm programs ever—a package that became a central part of the Roosevelt administration's New Deal. Wallace's approach was to provide incentives for farmers to cut back on production while markets were glutted and prices were low. His plan for an "ever normal granary" enabled farmers to protect their markets by storing surplus grain in times of bumper crops. They were allowed to borrow from the federal government against their stored harvests. When production was down and prices were higher, they could then profitably sell their grain and pay off their loans. This ingenious approach worked and is a prime reason that Henry A. Wallace is acknowledged by many as the most important agricultural leader of the twentieth century. His system, or some version of it, was the basic agricultural law of the land from the mid-1930s for the next sixty years until Congress terminated it, I think unwisely, in 1996. The Freedom to Farm Act of that year *did* give farmers more freedom to plant as much grain as they wished, but it left them with no price stabilization system. Once acreage restrictions were lifted, surpluses mounted, and in the absence of any price support floor, farm prices collapsed. I have heard more than a few farmers describe this congressional action as the Freedom to Go Broke Act.

As a youth in South Dakota, I saw anxious parents trying to stretch scarce dollars to feed their families. I also saw the steady stream of hoboes who came to our door asking for food. My father and mother never once said no to these young men, who were riding the rails looking for work. But not until I arrived in Italy in 1944 had I seen the kind of hunger that stunts young bodies and can end lives prematurely.

In September that year, I was on board a troopship as it eased into Naples harbor. In the approach to the docking area, I could see scores of Italian children lining up and shouting to us to throw Hershey bars, Babe Ruths, and Wrigley's gum. At this point the ship's captain broke in over the loudspeaker and ordered us not to throw anything to the youngsters. He explained that children in war-torn Italy were hungry—on the edge of starvation—and that a few days earlier, when American troops had thrown candy from an incoming ship, some of it fell into the water and a number of children had drowned scrambling for it.

I served in Italy for the next year as a bomber pilot, hitting targets in Nazi Germany and the oil refineries of Eastern Europe. Frequently I awakened to the sound of Italian mothers scratching through our garbage dumps for scraps of food.

This was the beginning of my lifelong interest in finding a practical formula for using the surplus production of American farmers to feed needy people in America and around the world. Such a plan could strengthen the markets of our farmers while feeding the hungry. A decade after my experiences in wartime Italy, I was elected to Congress with the first opportunity to translate my ideas on agriculture and feeding the hungry into public policy.

In the 1950s, after the war, large surpluses of grain accumulated in American storage facilities. The secretary of agriculture, Ezra Taft Benson, began to speak publicly of "burdensome surpluses" as the source of a serious American farm problem. I had a different view. It seemed to me in the 1950s, as it does now, that farm surpluses could be a blessing rather than a curse. It is true that without positive, imaginative action, surplus crops would depress market prices to the point where farmers would be unable even to recover the cost of production. This is the route to bankruptcy, mortgage foreclosures, and an agricultural depression that is damaging to the national economy. The serious troubles in the farm belt during the 1920s helped bring on the 1929 collapse of the New York stock market and the Great Depression of the 1930s. When farmers quit buying tractors, cars, appliances, tires, clothing, paint, lumber, and a host of other items, the entire economy is dampened. But if the government were prepared to purchase the surplus part of the crop and distribute it carefully to hungry people in our own country and abroad, we could both protect the markets of our farmers and reduce the number of hungry people.

With the Cold War over and defense spending down, the U.S. government has its first budget surplus since 1963. Some of this surplus could be used to meet the cost of bolstering our farm economy and feeding the hungry. In this kind of effort, we would need to be careful not to disrupt the commercial markets of other farmers and exporters, both in the United States and abroad. Nations that produce surplus grain, including Canada, Australia, France, and, in due course, India, China, and Russia, should be enlisted to share their abundance with the world's hungry. Developed countries that do not have farm surpluses could contribute cash, shipping, field personnel, utensils, processed foods, and other things needed in a well-planned feeding program.

As matters now stand, according to the most recent estimate of the UN Food and Agriculture Organization, slightly fewer than 800 million people around the world suffer from hunger. Most of them live in rural areas of the developing countries. They depend on farming for both their food and their income. To attack the world's hunger, we must move on two fronts: first, we must institute direct special feeding programs especially for schoolchildren and pregnant and nursing mothers and their infants; second, we must improve local agricultural practices.

Women should be given the opportunity to play a central role both in the direct feeding programs and in the production of food. A number of studies by the World Food Program in Bangladesh, Angola, and other Third World countries have demonstrated that women are more likely than men to budget and handle food resources carefully. The children in a family are more likely to be fed well if their mothers are in charge of the food.

I suggest the following five-point program:

(1) *I would like to see America take the lead in working toward a school lunch program that embraces every child in the world.* Such a program is well within the reach of the international community. We, and other countries, have the food resources and the know-how to establish and maintain such a program. There is no practical reason why any child should go hungry anywhere in the world.

While writing this book I discussed the concept of a universal school lunch program with President Clinton at the White House on May 26, 2000. Knowing how intensely busy the President is, I had expected only ten or fifteen minutes of his time. Instead he assembled his top assistants—White House Chief of Staff John Podesta, national security advisor Sandy Berger, economic advisor Gene Sperling, Secretary of Agriculture Dan Glickman, Deputy Aid Administrative Hattie Babbitt, a top executive from the Budget Bureau, and Congressman James McGovern of Massachusetts, who has long been interested in the issue of hunger.

The animated discussion lasted for an hour and a half with the President obviously fascinated by the idea and asking frequent questions. When I finished my presentation, he struck the cabinet room table in front of him and exclaimed, "This is just simply a grand idea! I want us to go forward with it."

True to his word, on July 23, 2000, while attending the G-8 Summit in Okinawa, Japan, President Clinton announced to the seven other heads of state that the United States will take the lead in establishing a school lunch program for the world's children. The President then committed an additional $300 million, largely in farm surpluses, to launch the effort in its first year. He invited other nations to join in this effort.

Then on July 27, 2000, Senator Richard Lugar of Indiana, chairman of the U.S. Senate Agriculture Committee, scheduled a public hearing on the international school lunch proposal and invited former senator Robert Dole and me to be the lead-off witnesses. Senator Dole and I testified as a team, which lent a strong bipartisan flavor to the hearing. As former presidential nominees of our respective parties, we had also established an effective bipartisan coalition in the Senate on matters related to agriculture and nutrition. While still testing the universal lunch idea with my colleagues in Rome, in the spring of 2000, I telephoned Bob Dole in Washington and asked him if he could support my effort. After asking a few questions, he said that he would be proud to team up with me on the proposal. He was the first person I called in the United States. It has been reassuring and most helpful to have his support. Our former Senate colleagues gave us the warmest, most supportive reception that I have ever witnessed at a congressional hearing.

Senator Tom Harkin of Iowa, the ranking Democrat on

the committee, observed that "your idea is so compelling and so morally and economically sound that I wonder why we didn't think of it a long time ago."

Senator Tom Daschle, the Democratic Leader of the Senate, came to the hearing to register a ringing endorsement of the proposal as did the other South Dakota senator, Tim Johnson, who has developed a keenly informed knowledge of hunger issues.

Senator Patrick Leahy of Vermont, a longtime member of the Agriculture Committee, was equally forceful in his support of an international school lunch program. Chairman Lugar planned and conducted the hearing admirably. Also on the Republican side was a man with whom I once served on the committee, Thad Cochran of Mississippi. He also lent his support to the lunch idea.

Senator Richard Durbin of Illinois and Congressman McGovern followed Senator Dole and me to the witness stand—they've been supporters of the school lunch concept from the moment that they first heard it mentioned. Then came supportive testimony from Dan Glickman and the director of the UN World Food Program, Catherine Bertini. These two people will play crucial roles in supplying, funding, and administrating the program. Working in concert with them will be the private voluntary agencies such as Catholic Relief Service, Church World Service, Lutheran World Relief, the Joint Distribution Committee, Bread for the World, CARE, and America's Second Harvest. Witnesses from these agencies completed the Agriculture Committee hearing. I stress that we can't operate a universal school lunch program effectively without the richly experienced and highly motivated participation of the private voluntary agencies around the world.

Of the world's hungry people, 300 million are school-age children. Not only do they bear the pangs of hunger but also their malnutrition leads to loss of energy, listlessness, and vulnerability to diseases of all kinds. Hungry children cannot function well in school—if, indeed, they are able to attend school at all. Hunger and malnutrition in childhood years can stunt the body and mind for a lifetime. Every minute, more than ten children under the age of five die of hunger. No one can even guess at the vastly larger number of older children and adults who lead damaged lives because of malnutrition in their fetal or infant days.

A nutritious, balanced school lunch for every child is the best investment we can make in the health, education, and global society of the future. After President John Kennedy appointed me in 1961 to head the U.S. Food for Peace program, I was contacted by a remarkable Catholic priest who was stationed with the Maryknoll Fathers in the impoverished Puno area of Peru. Father Dan McClellan convinced me that if the United States could supply the food, the Maryknoll Fathers could administer a school lunch program in the Puno region.

On May 12, 1961, Prime Minister Pedro Beltran of Peru came to my office at the White House to place his signature on an agreement for school lunches for 30,000 Puno students, to be administered by the Maryknoll Fathers. At the prime minister's suggestion, however, the food was given to the children as a breakfast, upon their arrival at school. Mr. Beltran told us that the children did not receive enough food at home to begin the day. A school breakfast would be an incentive for students to be on time and would give them enough energy for the day's educational activities. Perhaps a glass of milk with a cookie or a piece of bread could be added at midday as an energy pickup.

In the Puno area of Peru, illiteracy was 90 percent. Only

a meager fraction of the students were in school. In some schools, nine out of ten students dropped out before completing the sixth grade. Schoolchildren were seriously handicapped by the lethargy and drowsiness that resulted from malnutrition. But within six months after the U.S.-assisted school lunch program began in the fall of 1961, teachers noted that attendance had nearly doubled and academic performance had improved dramatically.

The signing by Prime Minister Beltran and me signaled a new emphasis in Food for Peace on U.S.-assisted school feeding programs. This was the first U.S. agreement of this kind. By 1964, 12 million, or one out of three, schoolchildren in South America were being fed a nutritious daily lunch through Food for Peace.

President Kennedy launched the Alliance for Progress in 1961. It was a cooperative effort on the part of the United States and the states of Latin America to raise the standard of living in Latin America. I observed at the time that "the most important resource of Latin America or of any continent and the one which holds the key to the future is children. Unless the children of Latin America can develop into healthy, educated citizens, the Alliance for Progress will amount to very little. That is why the expanding Food for Peace program focused more and more on the child-feeding programs. No part of the Alliance for Progress efforts was more important." (Food for Peace was a separate White House initiative that was launched before the Alliance for Progress, but we coordinated our efforts with the Alliance.)

What better investment could we make than locating a competent institution to manage and monitor a school breakfast or lunch program, which we could then confidently supply with our surplus foods?

Shortly after I began directing the Food for Peace program around the world, the dean of the University of Georgia telephoned my White House office. He told me that in his opinion the federal school lunch program had done more than any other federal program to advance the development of the South.

The school lunch program was launched in 1946, just after the Second World War. The wartime draft had revealed that a shocking number of young American men were ineligible for military service because of poor health—much of which appeared to be diet-related. Congress acted in considerable part because it became convinced that the poor health of much of our youth—especially in the South—threatened our national security. This concern was enough to convince even vigorous conservatives, traditionally opposed to more federal involvement in the schools, that school lunches should be an exception to the rule. Senator Richard Russell of Georgia and President Harry Truman were key players in establishing the School Lunch Program. The Georgia dean, a thoughtful lifetime educator, gave the federal school lunch program major credit for improving the physical strength, the mental alertness, the athletic ability, the self-confidence, and the productivity of the youth of the South. "If I had to preserve one federal program above all others, I would still choose the school lunch program," the dean said. It should be noted that until 1968 children were required to pay most of the cost of their lunches. Senator Dole and I were instrumental in passing legislation that provided free or reduced price lunches for poor children.

In Asia, Africa, and Latin America, wherever we have experimented with school lunches, we have seen school attendance double in a year or so; grades have also climbed. A daily lunch is the surest magnet for drawing children to school that anyone has yet devised. This is a very important fact because of the world's 300 million school-age children, 130 million are illiterate and not attending school. If education is the key to development in the Third World, the school lunch is the key to unlocking the education door. Of the 130 million not attending school most are girls because of favoritism toward boys. These illiterate girls marry at the age of eleven, twelve, or thirteen and and have an average of six children. Girls who go to school marry later and have an average of 2.9 children. A good school lunch is the best way yet found to get both girls and boys into school. The lowly school lunch indirectly produces healthier youngsters, advances education, reduces the birthrate, and provides a profitable market for the surplus farm commodities of the United States and other surplus-producing countries.

A school lunch every day for every child in the world would require the labor and initiative of many people and nations. In the United States, we would need to call on churches, synagogues, and mosques, as well as our secular philanthropic groups. Such religious and charitable institutions are already engaged in administering and distributing food relief abroad. But they should be urged and enabled to do much more. Wherever such private agencies can take the place of government in administering and monitoring school lunches or other food programs, they should be encouraged to do so. Also, wherever possible, local farmers should be given an opportunity to supply food at a fair price to the local school lunch program. When locally produced food is available, food aid can be acquired more cheaply from recipient or neighboring countries than from more distant sources where shipping and handling charges would be significant. The program will still require substantial dairy, livestock, and cereal grain production from the United States and other surplus-producing countries, because local supplies are not always equal to the demand. Beyond this, private foundations, labor unions, corporations and individuals should consider contributing to this cause. Such contributions should go to the UN World Food Program in Rome.

I would estimate the start-up costs covering the first two years of a school lunch program seriously intended to be universal at $3 billion. With the United States initially in the lead, our portion might reach half of that figure—$1.5 billion spread out over two years. The bulk of that would be in surplus commodities purchased in the American market: Texas and Montana livestock; Kansas wheat; South Dakota corn and hogs; Arkansas and North Carolina poultry; California and Florida oranges; Wisconsin and New York dairy products; Washington, Oregon, and Massachusetts cranberries and fish; Idaho and Maine potatoes.

As more and more students enrolled in the program, costs would increase, but we may hope that more and more countries would join in helping to finance the program, so American costs would probably not increase significantly, if at all. Also, expected contributions from private foundations, corporations, labor unions, and individuals should hold down government costs.

It is my hope that the receiving governments would themselves be able to take over and finance the program within five or six years. Meanwhile, the program would be under the instructional and monitoring eyes of the World Food Program, which has highly capable and experienced people in field offices within eighty countries.

(2) A second nutritional program that I would like to see go worldwide is the American Special Supplemental Food

Program for Women, Infants and Children. This program, known as WIC ("Women, Infants, and Children") provides food, nutrition counseling, and access to health services for low-income pregnant and breast-feeding women, other postpartum women, and infants and young children who are at nutritional risk.

I had the privilege of cosponsoring the legislation establishing WIC in 1972, with the late Senator Hubert Humphrey and Senator Bob Dole. The program has been a dramatic success in the United States, significantly improving the health and well-being of millions of young mothers and their children. In doing so it has reduced the cost of Medicaid and other medical programs.

Given our experience with WIC, Americans could lead the way in extending this program abroad, through the United Nations. Along with a universal school lunch program, an international WIC system would offer a mighty one-two punch against world hunger. And here again, American farmers, ranchers, and dairymen would benefit, along with producers in other countries.

I estimate the start-up cost for an international WIC program at $1 billion for the first two years. With the United States in the lead, our cost would be $500 million spread over two years. As with the universal school lunch program, costs would rise as more and more needy young mothers and their infants were drawn into the vitally important WIC program. And again, I anticipate that the participation of other UN member states would make unnecessary further increases in the U.S. portion of the cost.

Some of my colleagues in Rome are a little more skeptical about the operation of a WIC program abroad than they are about school lunch programs. They point out that the schoolhouse and its faculty and administrative staff provide a structure for feeding students; no such structure exists for young mothers and their infants. One possible answer is to set aside one hour a day when a school classroom could be used for WIC recipients. Where there is a church or a public meeting room, it may offer an alternative location. Mothers could be given food rations to take home for the weekend.

(3) A third step in the battle against world hunger could be the establishment of food reserves around the globe. The biblical story of Joseph in Egypt building a granary to store bountiful grain harvests for use in poor years is still a valid lesson. Countries producing grain surpluses should be encouraged to store the surplus against the day when crop failures, droughts, or international emergencies call on it. In the developing world, with less experience in modern grain storage, reserve storage facilities could be improved and expanded and then closely monitored by the UN Food and Agriculture Organization to prevent neglect or mishandling.

(4) A fourth step could be the fundamental long-term instrument in the war against hunger: assisting developing states to improve their own farm production, food processing, and food distribution. Most people in Asia, Africa, Latin America, and the Middle East live on farms or in rural villages. Agriculture is their physical and economic lifeline. Many of them are still farming with methods and equipment little improved since ancient times.

One ingredient in the amazing success of American agriculture has been the technical help and improved farming methods offered farmers by the land-grant colleges, including research on seeds, soil conservation, better cultivation practices, pesticides, and water usage. Agricultural experiment stations and county extension agents have also advised farmers on improved production methods. Such know-how could greatly lift the production and standards of life in the developing world. How could it be supplied?

I would suggest a Farmers Corps, patterned after the Peace Corps. Retired farmers in the United States and other developed countries could be recruited and paid a modest salary to go abroad for six months or more to teach improved farming methods. Each country would pay the cost of its own Corps. Many farmers who have retired for reasons of age or health are at a loss for how to use their retirement years. The Farmers Corps could provide a satisfying and adventurous outlet for such farmers. Some years ago, a treasured South Dakota friend of mine, my wife Eleanor's uncle, Harlan Payne, retired after a lifetime of farming. Restless, feeling useless, depressed in his retirement, he committed suicide. I believe that the Farmers Corps could have saved this good man's life while helping other farmers abroad. He would have loved all of that. Farm women, too, with their years of hard work and varied experience as partners in managing the farm, would have valuable wisdom to share.

Young men and women who have grown up on farms in the United States and other developed countries might also wish to do a stint in the Farmers Corps. As farms have grown larger, there are fewer opportunities for individual ownership for the sons and daughters of farmers. The Farmers Corps could provide a transition for such young people, who would also gain a new experience in a wider world.

A Farmers Corps should be administered by the Food and Agriculture Organization of the United Nations. As with other UN initiatives, the United States would be expected to pay 25 percent of the cost. Congress, of course, would have to authorize this expenditure. The American members of the Corps could be recruited and prepared for overseas service by the U.S. Department of Agriculture.

(5) A promising fifth weapon in the war against world hunger is the emergence of high-yield scientific agriculture, including genetically modified crops. The gene modification controversy has obscured its promise. Legitimate questions have been raised about some aspects of the use of chemicals in livestock. These questions deserve honest, scientifically sound answers. But the biotechnical improvement of both the quality and quantity of animals and plants is a major breakthrough in the battle against global hunger. That scientific breakthrough enables life-sustaining plants to survive pests, salt, and dry weather—all with less reliance on pesticides and irrigation water. Cereal grains can be modified to mature more quickly and yet have more nutritional benefits.

Some of the earlier successes with modifying plant genes have resulted in plants with greater resistance to insects. Since such plants require less pesticide, they improve farm income while reducing environmental damage.

Research is also moving ahead by Swiss scientists to produce a more nutritious strain of rice, a crop that feeds nearly 2.5 billion people. With increased Vitamin A and iron content, this newly modified rice could potentially prevent millions of cases of blindness and anemia among children. The modified rice is better for the overall health of youngsters.

Every new scientific breakthrough has been greeted over the centuries by skepticism, fear, and hostility. Such reactions are not all bad and, indeed, can be productive: they may force a measure of caution and proof before new methods and techniques are accepted. There must be more research, experimentation, and discussion before the final word is reached on the emerging biotechnology in agriculture.

The Food and Agriculture Organization of the United Nations has now established an intergovernmental group of experts to look into critical issues related to biotechnology, including risk assessment, labeling, and standards for international trade. Through this group, some of the best minds in the world can conduct a searching inquiry into genetically modified crops. The FAO has no ax to grind, no agenda but to arrive at the most realistic assessment possible of all aspects of this issue.

What we do know already is that for the past century science and technology have played a key role in greatly augmenting the production of American farmers and those in other advanced countries. The hybrid seed corn developed scientifically by Henry Wallace and his family in Iowa after 1926 was a valuable breakthrough, not only for Iowa farmers, but for farmers around the world.

The "Green Revolution," which began in 1968, got its name after scientists discovered through gene modification how to increase the capacity of green plants to use sunlight, water, and soil nutrients. This breakthrough essentially made it possible to grow more food on less land with fewer pesticides and less water.

Since the 1960s most of the increase in food production—notably, an estimated three-fourths of the increase has come in India and other parts of South Asia—has stemmed from the Green Revolution. To the best of my knowledge, no one has been poisoned or sickened by these modified crops. Indeed, the health of people and livestock consuming modified grains has improved. The Green Revolution and other crop modifications will continue to be the source of food production increases in the next thirty years if farmers proceed with modern scientific agriculture. This should be good for farmers, good for consumers, and good for the environment.

It was the technology of farm machinery and the use of science to modify plants that enabled food producers to head off the prediction by Thomas Malthus that population growth would outstrip increases in food production. But as we move into the twenty-first century, population continues to grow, with shrinking per capita arable land and irrigation possibilities. I believe that genetically engineered crops may be an indispensable instrument in the war against hunger, by increasing both the quality and the quantity of food produced per acre. If so, we need to discuss openly and fairly the fears and risks, as well as the hopes and values, of scientific farming.

Thus far, most genetically altered crops—three fourths of the world's total harvest—have been grown in the United States, a source of anxiety in France and a few other countries. We need to promote a continuing dialogue with our European friends and the American public about all aspects of the issue.

Meanwhile, we should keep in mind that for more than four decades, the United States and other countries have helped keep millions of our fellow humans alive because science has enabled us to achieve a much higher output of corn, rice, wheat, and potatoes. We have shared our technology of production widely with the developing world, including the small, impoverished farmers of Asia, Africa, and Latin America. Scientific agriculture has made American farmers the envy of the world. I believe that the new genetic developments will prove vital in equipping farmers to win the war against world hunger.

Dr. Norman Borlaug, the Nobel Prize–winning Distinguished Professor of International Agriculture at Texas A & M University, writing in the March 15, 2000, issue of the *International Herald Tribune,* declares: "Science and technology are under attack in affluent nations, where misinformed environmentalists claim that the consumer is being poisoned by high-yielding systems of agricultural production, including genetically modified crops."

I count myself a Borlaug fan. The father of the Green Revolution, he is an esteemed socially conscious scientist. But I must confess that some of my grandchildren disagree with Dr. Borlaug and me about genetically modified crops. The headline on the Borlaug article I have quoted reads: "Biotechnology Will Be the Salvation of the Poorest." Not so, contend some of my bright grandchildren. Biotech and gene modification will ruin the poorest, the richest, and those in between, they say. Why? Because, they argue, such technologies disrupt the natural growth of crops and no one can be certain of the long-range results in our bodies of such manipulation of nature's food.

Some would be so cruel as to suggest that my grandchildren are smarter than their grandfather—that they might even be smarter than Dr. Borlaug. I come back at them with the eternal response of old people to young people: "Where is your respect for the wisdom of us old guys?" But usually I reply with an answer that carries more weight with grandchildren: "The jury is still out on genetic farming. Let's wait for the final verdict." I don't add what I'm thinking: "And then you'll see that I am right and you are wrong!"

Without the application of these new and better farming methods, the task of defeating hunger becomes more difficult and less certain of victory. There is reason to believe that recently developed scientific farming methods can reduce farmers' costs, increase their production, safeguard the environment, and provide more food for the hungry.

In defending scientific farming against the criticisms of the more extreme environmentalists, Dr. Borlaug further notes: "Were Asia's 1961 average cereal yields of 930 kilograms per hectare to still prevail today, nearly 600 million hectares of additional land of the same quality would have been needed to equal the 1997 cereal harvest. Obviously, such a surplus of land was not available in Asia. Moreover, even if it were, think of the soil erosion, loss of forests and grasslands, wildlife species that would have occurred had we tried to produce these larger harvests with low technology."

If the reader will allow another quote from Dr. Borlaug, I urge its careful consideration: "Thirty years ago, in my acceptance speech for the Nobel Peace Prize, I said that the Green Revolution had won a temporary victory in man's war against hunger, which if fully implemented, could provide sufficient food for humankind through the end of the 20th century. . . .

"I now say that the world has the technology . . . to feed a population of 10 billion people. The more pertinent question today is whether farmers and ranchers will be permitted to use this new technology.

"Extreme environmental elitists seem to be doing everything they can to stop scientific progress. Small, well-financed, vociferous, anti-science groups are threatening the development and application of new technology, whether it is developed from biotechnology or more conventional methods of agricultural science."

It is probably true that affluent countries can afford to reject scientific agriculture and pay more for foods produced by so-called natural methods. But the 800 million poor, chronically hungry people of Asia, Africa, and Latin America cannot afford such foods. If scientific agriculture had not been introduced to parts of these poor continents three or four decades ago, millions of people now alive would have died. If further efforts to bring the advantages of science to developing countries are thwarted by ill-advised critics, millions of poor people will pay a painful price—perhaps making the ultimate sacrifice, of life itself.

SHORTLY AFTER I set down my thoughts on the possible role of biotechnology in delivering humanity from hunger, *Time* magazine editors and scientific writers devoted much of their July 31, 2000, issue to a cover story on this vital subject. The article included statements from some of the world's most renowned scientists who support the genetic modifications of grains, as well as criticisms from some environmentalists.

Time's cover carried the picture of Ingo Potrykus, a Swiss scientist and professor at the Swiss Federal Institute of Technology in Zurich, who has been working for years in his laboratory and in the field to alter crops so that they become more nutritious, more resistant to pests, rot, and disease, and require less water, pesticide, and fertilizer. In recent years he has concentrated his experiments on rice with the collaboration of another distinguished scientist, Professor Peter Beyer of the University of Freiburg. These two scientists and others were aware that half of the world's 6 billion people depend on rice as their major dietary staple. *Time's* editors concluded that "these people were so poor that they ate a few bowls of rice a day and almost nothing more." The scientists' investigations demonstrated that the rice diet of the world's poor was deficient in vitamin A—so much so that it is causing a million children to die annually.

With these grim facts to spur them on, Potrykus and Beyer sought an acceptable way to modify rice so that it would contribute to the health of children rather than contributing to their blindness and deaths. After seven years of diligent research and experimentation with the expenditure of $2.6 million supplied by the Rockefeller Foundation, the Swiss government, and the European Union, they found the answer. It came in the form of modified rice that has come to be known as "golden rice" because of its yellow color in contrast to the whitish color of conventional rice. Golden rice supplies the vitamin A, the iron, and the overall nutritional enrichment that is lacking in conventional rice.

Despite its life-enhancing qualities, the new rice had been assailed by some environmentalists in Europe, followed by a small but vocal minority in the United States. Potrykus, himself an environmentalist, had been dismayed by the attack on his scientific findings. "It would be irresponsible," he told *Time,* "not to say immoral, not to use biotechnology to solve this problem."

As the *Time* editors point out, by the year 2020, the global demand for grain is "projected to go up by nearly half, while the amount of arable land available to satisfy that demand will not only grow much more slowly but also, in some areas, will probably dwindle. Add to that the need to conserve overstressed water resources and reduce the use of polluting chemicals, and the enormity of the challenge becomes apparent."

Gordon Conway, an agricultural ecologist and environmentalist who heads the Rockefeller Foundation, is baffled, like every other scientist I have interviewed or read, by those environmentalists who object to genetically modified plants and gains. Conway told the *Time* research team that "21st century farmers will have to draw on every arrow in their agricultural quiver, including genetic engineering. And contrary to public perception, those who have the least to lose and the most to gain are not well-fed Americans and Europeans but the hollow-bellied citizens of the developing world."

In the United States, the opposition to genetic farming is trying to pressure the federal government into requiring that all foods containing genetically modified grains be labeled. This would embrace 70 percent of all the processed food in American supermarkets. This federal intervention is now gathering strength in Congress. My first reaction on hearing about the food labeling movement was that it is an unnecessary nuisance for industry and another increase in the cost of food, but if it will ease the minds of protesters why not do it. But as Gene Grabowski told *Time:* "Our data show that 60% of consumers would consider a mandatory biotech label as a warning that it is unsafe." Dan Eramion, a spokesman for the Biotechnology Industry Organization, added: "It is easier to scare people about biotechnology than to educate them."

After reading widely on the potential role of scientific farming, including the genetic input, I am convinced that if the world does not move forward on this front, untold millions of people will die as a consequence. I have for years admired the principles and policies of such environmental groups as the Sierra Club and the Friends of the Earth. I believe most of the officers and members of these and similar groups have long endorsed my public positions. But I believe their opposition to biotechnology as the newly emerging handmaiden of agriculture is both ill-founded and threatening to human survival in the poor countries of our planet. I propose a bargain to my dissenting environmental friends: I will continue to read any literature you make available to me on the dangers of genetically modified grains and other foods if you will read carefully the findings and reasonings of Professors Potrykus and Beyer.

I would only like to add a note of caution to those trying to prevent the use of biotechnology in the struggle of third-world countries to feed their people. Consider these words from Nigeria's minister of agriculture, Hassan Adamu: "It is possible to kill someone with kindness, literally. That could be the result of the well-meaning but extremely misguided attempts by Europeans and North American groups that are advising Africans to be wary of agricultural biotechnology. They claim to have the environment and public health at the core of their opposition, but scientific evidence disproves their claims that enhanced crops are anything but safe. If we take their alarmist warnings to heart, millions of Africans will suffer and possibly die" (*The Washington Post,* September 11, 2000).

IN 1996 the World Food Summit convened in Rome under the auspices of the UN Food and Agriculture Organization. Virtually every country on earth was represented, many by prime ministers and heads of state. After extensive deliberation, the conference resolved to reduce human hunger by half by the year 2015. By this goal, the 800 million people suffering from hunger in 1996 would be reduced to 400 million in the next 15 years—a reduction of 27 million annually.

This is a difficult and complicated goal, but a reasonable and practical one. I believe that if the United States and the international community will adopt the five steps I suggest for feeding the hungry, we could go further; we could eliminate all hunger within another 15 years, by 2030. The five-step formula will also promote prosperity for the farmers of America and other surplus-producing countries, including France, Canada, Australia, and Argentina. What could be a greater achievement than to free the world of the ancient scourge of hunger during the first three decades of the new millennium?

There will, of course, be problems, concerns, and risks involved in ending world hunger while maintaining the prosperity of farmers, livestockmen, and dairymen, respecting commercial markets, and preserving the global environment. These and other issues will be dealt with in the pages that follow. Understandably, some of the economic and social issues will prove controversial. But one compelling moral issue is clear: every major religion and ethical system commands its adherents to feed the hungry. There is no room in Christianity, Judaism, Islam, Buddhism, Hinduism, or any of the other great traditions for those who turn their backs on the hungry. We should feed the hungry because it is right to do so. I believe this undertaking will enrich us all, but we should do this regardless of economic advantage to ourselves because it is the right thing to do.

In the battle against hunger and poverty it is easy to retire to the sidelines, complaining that not much can be done. But as Pope John Paul II told the UN Food and Agriculture Organization on November 18, 1999: "What is needed is the more profound and infinitely more creative power of hope." If we follow that spirit, said the Pope, we can realize the promise of the Scriptures: "He hath filled the hungry with good things" (Luke 1:53). To which we might add the insight of the great former secretary general of the United Nations, Sweden's Dag Hammarskjöld: "In our own era, the road to holiness necessarily passes through the world of action" (Hammarskjöld, *Markings*, p. xxi).

CHAPTER 2

FOOD FOR PEACE

IN SEEKING THE WAY to a world free from hunger, it may be well to recall one of the brightest and most successful initiatives ever taken by the United States: the Food for Peace Program. Launched in the Eisenhower administration during the 1950s, the effort was given dramatic new force in the Kennedy administration during the 1960s.

The creative and highly commendable Peace Corps, brilliantly directed by Sargent Shriver during the Kennedy administration, deservedly received high praise for its work around the world. Not so well known is that Food for Peace quietly saved more lives and contributed more to the economic and social development of people around the globe.

The program brought food to an estimated one billion hungry people in Asia, Africa, Latin America, and the Middle East. It did so in a variety of ways: (1) grain sales on favorable terms to needy countries; (2) direct food donations, sometimes distributed by religious and charitable organizations, including Church World Service, Catholic Relief Services, the Joint Jewish Distribution Committee, Lutheran World Relief, the Quakers, the Mennonite Central Kitchen, CARE, and others; (3) school lunch programs; and (4) "food for wages," under which workers received part of their wages in food while they were engaged in building roads, irrigation systems, water and sewage systems, health clinics, and schools.

Food for Peace had its origins in one of the most imaginative pieces of legislation ever enacted by Congress, Public Law 480, which became law in 1954. This bipartisan, widely supported legislation was Congress's response to the increasingly costly government-held farm surpluses of the 1950s. Seeking to prevent surplus grain production from destroying market prices for farmers, the government agreed to help individual farmers by granting them loans against their stored surplus grain until it could be sold at a fair price, at which time the loans would be repaid. But as the surpluses grew, they depressed farm prices even as they lay in storage. Beyond this, the cost to the government of holding the grain off the market soon reached $1 billion annually. Also, some of the grain began to deteriorate, having been held too long.

Meanwhile, reports of human hunger in various parts of the world came to the attention of Congress and the American public. Why not initiate congressional action to authorize the shipment of American farm surpluses to the hungry areas of the world? The answer of Congress was Public Law 480, which is still on the books.

The law was a blend of economic self-interest and humanitarian reaction to global hunger. On the economic self-interest side were the following benefits. First, moving the grain from costly storage into the stomachs of hungry people helped to safeguard the farmers' market. Second, billion-dollar storage costs were slashed. Third, since Congress required that half of the grain (now 75 percent) being shipped abroad had to be moved in American vessels, the hard-pressed U.S. merchant marine benefited substantially.

American railroads and the trucking industry also profited from grain shipments across the country to the seaports. Fourth, much of the grain traveled to needy countries by way of concessional sales. The United States accepted payment in the "soft" local currencies of countries such as India, a major recipient of Food for Peace. The uses of the currency were then negotiated between the United States and the receiving country. A portion of it could be used by the United States for such purposes as the Fulbright student exchange program, expenses of the U.S. Embassy, or even the expenses of U.S. Congressmembers, traveling abroad on official missions.

The humanitarian benefits of Food for Peace were more obvious. The program saved *millions* of lives. It strengthened the bodies and minds of millions of infants and young children and their elders, and it enabled them to achieve happier, more abundant lives. By reducing the strain and disruption of gnawing hunger, Food for Peace lived up to its name, removing some causes of conflict and violence. It is easier for a society to move toward peace and freedom if its people are comfortable and well-fed.

Unfortunately, during the 1950s, what eventually was called Food for Peace did not carry this name or its substantive meaning. It was referred to as "surplus disposal," both within the government and outside. Some of the recipient countries began to see it as simply an American dumping operation to get rid of costly storages. This attitude was encouraged when the administrators forced Greece to accept unwanted tobacco while India was required to accept cotton, in each case as a condition for obtaining American food. The Greeks had their own sources of tobacco and the Indians had local supplies of cotton.

Hubert Humphrey deplored the narrow focus of the

program and its lack of any humanitarian and nutritional component. In April 1959 he designed new legislation, complete with a new name—"Food for Peace"—and a White House administrator. I was a young congressman at that time and the leader in the House of Representatives on Food for Peace. Like Senator Humphrey, I pointed out that it was an insult to hungry people to describe feeding them as "surplus disposal." It is acceptable to describe the garbage units in our kitchen sinks as disposal units; it is insensitive, if not insulting, to so describe feeding a child, a mother, or humankind in general. I called for a broader humanitarian focus and public interpretation of P.L. 480 with the name "Food for Peace." In House floor debate in 1958, I asked: "Can the President not see that, rather than a 'burden' to be deplored, agricultural abundance is one of America's greatest assets for raising living standards and promoting peace and stability in the free world?"

I also informed Congress that while I supported the grain storage program, the storages were climbing too high. By mid-1958 we would have over 1.3 billion bushels of corn and wheat, more than double our annual domestic requirement. I further noted that the annual storage cost would soon pass $1 billion. Why not make a broader, more humanitarian use of P.L. 480 to reduce our costs by feeding the hungry and building more stable and peaceful societies abroad?

With Humphrey in the Senate and me in the House keeping up a steady drumbeat on the need to broaden Food for Peace, momentum began to build in that direction during the late 1950s. Senator John Kennedy, the 1960 Democratic presidential nominee, was at first somewhat bored by agricultural issues. "I don't want to hear about agriculture from anyone but Ken Galbraith and I don't want to hear about it from him," he said, half-seriously, half-humorously. But the Humphrey-McGovern approach resonated with candidate Kennedy. The historian Thomas Knock of Southern Methodist University, who is nearing completion of a biography of me, has written that because it "linked an ostensibly unexciting domestic issue to foreign policy in a dynamic way, [it] helped him find his voice."

During his presidential campaign, I urged Kennedy to come to South Dakota, where I was making my first bid for the U.S. Senate. After introducing him to a huge throng of farmers at the National Plowing Contest near Sioux Falls, we got into his private plane to fly to my hometown, Mitchell. He had read to the crowd at Sioux Falls from a prepared text on agriculture. He knew that the speech had moved few if any listeners.

"What do you think I should do at Mitchell?" he asked. He was aware that several thousand people had been waiting inside the Mitchell Corn Palace for two hours to hear him. I suggested that he lay aside his farm speech and simply talk extemporaneously for a few minutes about how important our farmers and their abundant production are to America and to the world around us. Here is what he said to the audience in Mitchell: "I don't regard the agricultural surplus as a problem. I regard it as an opportunity to use [the food] imaginatively, not only for our own people, but for people all around the world." No group could do more for America, or the world, than farmers—not "if we recognize that food is strength, and food is peace, and food is freedom, and food is a helping hand to people around the world whose good will and friendship we want."

There was thunderous applause for these lines. They made every farmer feel that what he was doing was important to the nation and to the world. The farmer was now a vital part of American foreign policy in the far reaches of the globe.

Kennedy trumpeted those lines over and over during the fall campaign. In October, he appointed a committee to recommend ways that Food for Peace could be given both more permanence and a wider scope. He also wanted to see "a world food agency."

Thus, it was not surprising that on his third day in office and in his second Executive Order, Kennedy gave the Food for Peace Program a White House director, whom he ordered "to make a maximum effort to narrow the gap between abundance at home and near starvation abroad." The President added that the new director would make "the most vigorous and constructive use possible of American agricultural abundance."

I was highly honored when the President chose me to direct Food for Peace. Having preached the Food for Peace gospel during the previous decade with my friend and neighbor, Hubert Humphrey, I would have a glorious opportunity to make this concept a living reality around the world. Kennedy made the job easier by locating my office in the White House, thus keeping me out of the bureaucratic tangles of the Departments of Agriculture and State and other federal agencies. There are many brilliant and dedicated public servants in the various offices of the federal government, but I could not have accomplished the transformation of Food for Peace which the President wished had I been located anywhere other than the White House or the Executive Office of the President. Several government departments and agencies claimed a portion of the program—Agriculture, State, AID, Treasury, Commerce, and the Budget Bureau among them. Only a White House executive with presidential backing could have accelerated

Food for Peace agreements through this disparate array of federal offices, each understandably trying to protect its partial jurisdiction.

I told my staff during our first week in office that I did not want to hear the words "surplus disposal"—that we were in the business of feeding hungry children, not disposing of garbage. Anyone who wanted to be in the disposal business should apply to the D.C. sanitation department.

I said that we were under presidential order to expand the program, and this we were going to do. I couldn't say what the scope of the expansion would be, but I could say that it would be major.

I told them that we were going to transform Food for Peace into an important instrument of American foreign policy as it raised standards of living, produced better-nourished and therefore more capable students, and supported more stable and peaceful communities.

And we were not going to forget that all that we did in Food for Peace depended on the productivity of our farmers. There had been enough complaining about farm surpluses. There was no such thing as a "burdensome farm surplus" as long as there were hungry children in the world. So, I said, let's praise our farmers for their skill, hard work, and productivity and tell them that they make it possible for us to have the great privilege of feeding our fellow humans.

Farm surpluses, I said, "testified to the efficiency of our farmers, who comprised only 4 percent of the American populace and yet produced enough food to feed the other 96 percent plus millions of people abroad. By contrast, the Soviet Union, our cold war competitor, with half of its population engaged in farming, was unable to feed the other half."

The Soviet leader, Nikita Khrushchev, was quick to

concede his admiration of American agriculture, even as his military strategists planned to match us missile for missile. When he came to Washington, D.C., in 1959 at the invitation of President Eisenhower, the President asked him if there were points of interest he would like to see, including, if he wished, some of our military installations. The Russian premier expressed no enthusiasm for an inspection of our armaments. Instead, he asked permission to visit Disneyland and an Iowa corn and hog farm operated by two prominent brothers, Roswell and Jonathan Garst, who had corresponded with the Soviet leader. I have always suspected that if Khrushchev and I held any opinion in common, it was this: the chief American asset in our Cold War rivalry was not our weapons stockpile, but the dramatic superiority of our farmers and ranchers.

Early in the new administration, I recommended a series of Food for Peace missions to Latin America, Asia, and Africa to appraise local needs at first hand and consider how we could best respond. President Kennedy announced in his first State of the Union address that he was sending me to Argentina and Brazil. This made mine the first overseas mission of any kind by the new administration. Two memories of this tour have stayed with me and with Arthur Schlesinger, Jr., the President's special assistant, who accompanied me.

The first memory is of the hunger, poverty, and misery of northeast Brazil. It was my first direct view of the conditions that prevail in so much of the Third World. As we walked into the villages, it was painful even to gaze at these desperately poor people. In one hut that we entered at noontime, an emaciated young mother sat on the mud floor with an infant resting in her lap. Another child had died of measles the day before. Youngsters suffering from malnutrition frequently die of measles, chickenpox, colds, flu, or other diseases that adequately fed children usually have no trouble in overcoming. We walked through villages where children died before our eyes from what appeared to us to be malnutrition, perhaps complicated by some childhood illness. In the Brazilian hut we first entered, three other sickly children lay around the mud floor. The mother, whom we judged to weigh not more than 60 pounds, was a shapeless, totally flat-chested little soul. She had tried to make her children look more presentable, but she was too weak and ill to accomplish her task. It appeared that whatever meager food was to be found went to the children. A young Brazilian economist, Celso Furtado, accompanied Schlesinger and me. He said, as he observed us looking at the young mother: "She is the symbol of the underdeveloped world."

I have never forgotten that dismal scene. I doubt that I would now be writing this book had it not been for that visit.

We saw another view in the Brazil of 1961, this one in the slums of beautiful Rio de Janeiro. We had been told about the drought-stricken part of the country, so that was not a complete surprise. But how could one of the most beautiful cities in the world, filled with gorgeous mansions, be surrounded by some of the most miserable slums imaginable? The huts of the northeast were made of mud bricks dried by the sun. In the ramshackle favelas skirting Rio de Janeiro, they were made of cardboard boxes, pieces of tin, discarded parts of wrecked cars—anything that could be patched together to provide protection from the rain or the blistering sun.

I recall one emaciated little two-year-old boy, covered with sores, reaching up from the floor of a pathetic cardboard shack in the favelas for consolation. These images, the haunted eyes, hollow faces, sick and suffering infants and children—they have remained with me. What Schlesinger and I saw in Brazil's northeast and in the favelas of Rio de Janeiro shocked us all the more in that we knew Brazil was one of the better-situated countries in the developing world. We were later to see these scenes, or worse, repeated again and again in Africa and Asia.

Shortly after our return from Brazil and the filing of reports with the President and the secretaries of state and agriculture, we shipped to Brazil 16,000 tons of corn and beans and enough dried milk to feed 2 million people for a year. The U.S. government paid the cost. In my report to the President I had recommended that we have two basic missions. In the short run, when faced with the kind of hunger crisis we found in Brazil, we should open up the doors of Food for Peace to distribute food—not for economic or political reasons, but because it was the morally proper thing to do.

The long-term purpose of Food for Peace, I argued, should be to encourage better farming methods so that people in the developing world could find a way to meet part or all of their own food needs. To encourage such improvement in Third World agriculture, I started a number of Food for Wages projects, including village irrigation projects, rural roadway building, and water and sewage projects, as well as other development efforts. Those who engaged in these projects received a considerable portion of their wages in American wheat flour, cornmeal, soybean oil, and dried milk.

The Eisenhower administration had started a single program of this kind in Tunisia and financed it with the shipment of 44,763 tons of grain. During the first six months of the Kennedy administration, we were able to ship six times that amount of food to projects in a number of countries. By October 1963, twenty-two countries were participating in Food for Wages, and the flow of Food for Peace development aid had reached a million tons. Food for Wages was providing partial payments for 700,000 workers engaged in building hospitals, schools, bridges, dams, and roads, as well as in reforestation, irrigation, and reclamation. All of this was a part of the U.S. foreign assistance budget—perhaps the most beneficial part of our aid to poor countries.

The sector of Food for Peace that was dearest to my heart was the school lunch program. I was familiar with the magnificent results of the American school lunch program, including its contribution to the physical and mental health of students, its stimulus to students to study and to learn, its creation of athletic capability, and its nutritional lessons that students might take to their homes and utilize throughout their lives.

When we began developing school lunch offerings in impoverished countries, the results were spectacular. School attendance doubled in some cases as students went to school in search of their one daily nutritious meal. Academic performance improved dramatically in every school where we established a well-managed program.

By the middle of 1962, 35 million children in Latin America, Asia, and Africa were receiving a daily school lunch. The results everywhere were highly successful. By 1964, children receiving Food for Peace school lunches numbered 1 million in Peru, 2 million in South Korea, 3.5 million in Egypt, 4.5 million in Brazil, 9 million in India, and over 10 million in Southeast Asia.

Surveying these results, Professor Knock concluded: "The Peace Corps not excepted, McGovern had superintended the single greatest humanitarian achievement of the Kennedy-Johnson era." This is a tribute not to me but to the enlightened government program I was given the privilege of directing. I have been in public life for most of my adulthood. During those years I have never seen a government program that was a better blend of self-interest and moral purpose than Food for Peace.

I shall always be proud to have been the Food for Peace director in the Kennedy administration during 1961 and 1962. In his soon-to-be-published biography of me, Professor Knock concludes that I "had coordinated the feeding of more hungry people than any other individual in American history."

During this period, I was given an audience in Rome with perhaps the greatest pope of the twentieth century, John XXIII. The Pope took my hands and said: "When your Maker asks: 'Have you fed the hungry?' you may answer, 'Yes.' " I have benefited from association with many religious leaders, but as a Protestant clergyman's son, I treasure this blessing of Pope John above all others. I hope it will weigh against some of my sins!

EARLY ON at Food for Peace, I became interested in the possibility of other countries joining with us in a multilateral effort. When I was invited to Rome by Dr. B. R. Sen, a brilliant agriculturist from India who was the director general of the UN Food and Agriculture Organization, I accepted the invitation with that in mind.

Dr. Sen had been talking for some time about the need for a world food program to distribute food to the hungry. In a sense he was trying to build the machinery for an internationally run Food for Peace–type program. Such a program would tap into the resources of all countries, not simply the United States or other countries acting unilaterally.

So in April 1961, I found myself in Rome accompanied by two senior experts, one from the State Department and the other from the Department of Agriculture, Ray Ioanes, a brilliant civil servant who headed the Foreign Agriculture Service. As we flew toward Rome, I asked Ioanes what we could do to help launch a "World Food Program." The problem was money, he said. No country had yet pledged any financial support.

What would it take to get the program started? I asked. Jokingly, he said: If you have a hundred million dollars in your pocket, you can get up on the conference floor Monday and offer the start-up money. Ray had been through enough budget battles to know that it would take a year or two at best to get $100 million in new money through the chain of command to final approval. But I was new in the administration, and so was our President. So I asked Ray to draft a serious proposal, which I would call in to the White House for the President's prompt consideration.

Ray's proposal, scratched out on a note pad after our Saturday morning arrival in Rome, called for me to get recognition at the opening of the conference on Monday and state that on behalf of the United States, we were prepared to offer $40 million of grain and would urge Congress to authorize an additional $10 million in cash. This offer was being made with the understanding that other countries would match the U.S. offer, for a total fund of $100 million.

This was the proposal I got cleared at the White House that weekend with the help of my deputy, James Symington (later to be elected to Congress), and the talented and influential White House counsel Ted Sorensen. My two travel companions from State and Agriculture could not believe it, and Dr. Sen and his colleagues were in visible shock when I made the offer Monday morning. But after a brief recess to determine whether my offer was serious, the conference approved the proposal, thus committing their nations to match it. This they later did, with Canada, Britain, and Holland in the lead. That was the beginning of the UN's World Food Program, which was officially established in 1962. Today it is the biggest humanitarian feeding organization in the world. In 1998 it fed 75 million people around the world. It is currently headed by the able Catherine Bertini of Illinois.

The World Food Program delivers 6.5 million tons of food annually across the world. This is 95 percent of the food aid distributed multilaterally, and more than all single-country contributions combined, including the U.S. Food for Peace program.

The World Food Program is the world's most exciting and dynamic food assistance program. When there are natural disasters—floods, droughts, hurricanes, earthquakes—it moves quickly to provide food relief. When there are man-made conflicts—wars, insurrections, ethnic struggles—the World Food Program is there to help the innocent bystanders. When multitudes of refugees stream across the land, homeless and hungry, the World Food Program is there. It is both difficult and sometimes dangerous for relief workers to distribute food in wartime to its intended recipients. The combatants are eager to get control of food from any source, so World Food Program officials must always be on guard.

In Rwanda, where a bloody conflict drove vast numbers of people to flee in the late 1990s, the World Food Program fed nearly a million refugees as they returned to their homes. The emphasis then shifted to food-for-work projects that led to the building of 11,748 houses, seed assistance to over 500,000 farmers, and 124 school gardens. The World Food Program also assisted 280 nutritional centers which benefited 60,000 people monthly. Sadly, three WFP workers were killed by a rival group while they were assisting a band of refugees.

When natural disasters struck North Korea in the mid-1990s, undermining already precarious food and agricultural conditions, the World Food Program responded by setting up a daily feeding operation for 2.6 million children aged seven and under. When Catherine Bertini was criticized by a few people for sending United Nations food to a communist-led country, she replied: "I can't say to a hungry five-year-old boy, 'We won't feed you because we don't like your government.'" Who can refute that sentiment?

In Iraq the "Oil for Food" program of the United Nations authorized Iraq to sell $2 billion worth of its oil every six months to purchase food and other essentials. The World Food Program was designated to distribute food to 3 million Iraqi citizens. The agency was also instructed to set up a network of observers across the country to see that the food reached its intended recipients. Persons concerned about the painful impact of the UN embargo on the people of Iraq can draw some reassurance from the knowledge that the World Food Program has been delivering 4 million tons of food annually to the country's hungriest people.

Where there are people chronically hungry and impoverished, the World Food Program provides daily rations. Some are put to work building clinics, schools, and community water and sewage systems. Part of their wages may come in the form of food. This is the Food for Wages program that originated with Food for Peace in 1961.

Food for Peace

The World Food Program gives special attention to the needs of women, infants, and children. In activities similar to the domestic U.S. WIC program, pregnant and nursing mothers and their infants are given supplemental nourishment and special instruction on nutritional guidelines. This program is motivated by the grim fact that nearly a third of the world's children under the age of five are vulnerable to chronic illness and premature death because of inadequate nutrition during their mother's pregnancy or in the first years after birth.

The World Food Program has fought hard to offset the discrimination against women that makes it difficult for women in some societies to gain equal access to food, travel, medical care, and employment. For example, officials and workers have encountered blatant discrimination against women and girls in Afghanistan. Since the 1980s, the World Food Program has been by far the largest food aid operation in this strife-torn country, and program officers have worked hard to get food to females despite rigid barriers set up by the male-dominated society.

Without jeopardizing the nutritional content of its daily food ration, the WFP has held its costs low. A typical food ration of cornmeal, vegetable oils, beans, peas, and lentils can be delivered for 15 cents daily. The basic foods, of course, are donated by the member countries of the United Nations.

All in all, I believe that the World Food Program has proved to be a great human investment. I draw deep satisfaction from knowing that in 1961 I was privileged to make the U.S. offer that launched this program the following year. From its beginning in 1962, this international effort has operated with voluntary support from member governments. Each government decides how much it will contribute in cash and commodities. Last year's contributions totalled $1.7 billion, of which the U.S. provided a little over half, largely in commodities. The program has a worldwide force of 5,021 employees. Of these, 712 are professionals, 86 of them Americans. The program is not only the UN's major food arm, but also the single largest humanitarian project of the U.S. government.

THE OLDEST AND LARGEST of the UN specialized agencies is the Food and Agriculture Organization, founded in 1945 and based in Rome. One hundred and seventy-four countries—almost every nation in the world—are members of FAO. Whereas the UN World Food Program, founded in 1962, concentrates its major effort on direct feeding operations in emergency situations, with smaller uses of food aid for economic and social development, the Food and Agriculture Organization concentrates on long-term assistance to farmers in the developing world. In a sense, the FAO is a global application of the kinds of things the U.S. land-grant colleges, agricultural experiment stations, extension services, and the county agents do to assist American farmers.

The FAO was founded to improve the productivity of farmers in poor countries and generally to improve nutrition and the quality of life on the farms and in the rural villages where more than half the people of the world live. FAO farm experts, technicians, and scientists are engaged across the developing world, helping farmers to better manage their land, water, cultivation of crops, storage, and marketing.

The FAO is not only the major UN agency for agricultural development; it also has global jurisdiction over forestry and fisheries. FAO promotes fishing and the care of fishing resources because of the contribution fish provide to both income and diet.

The aquaculture promoted by FAO in Asia, Africa, and Latin America has tripled between 1984 and 1995 from less than 7 million tons of fish to 21.3 million tons. To the extent people can "farm the sea," they can add protein and healthy fats to the diets of their families and possibly have enough left over to sell or trade.

The FAO, in cooperation with the UN World Health Organization, works to improve the purity and safety of food by setting international food standards. These standards apply to over 200 commodities, while other standards set safe limits for over 3,000 contaminants.

The FAO has offered advice and technical assistance in improving forestry management in 90 countries. The widely respected David Harcharik, an American, was until recently the head of FAO's forestry programs. He has since been promoted to deputy director general of the entire FAO network.

The FAO is on the cutting edge of proper use of pesticides consistent with environmental values. Using integrated pest management, FAO technicians have demonstrated to Asian rice farmers that they can increase production and improve the quality of their rice while using smaller amounts of pesticide. Obviously, this is good for the environment; moreover, these new methods have saved Asian governments $150 million annually in pesticide subsidies. FAO has also been successful in underwriting campaigns to control crop-destroying locusts. Over $300 million has been invested in this valuable program, including a special effort in 1988 that protected crops in 40 African and Middle East countries against an especially heavy infestation. The locust invasions are reminiscent of the grasshopper swarms that were so destructive to American farms in the 1930s.

The FAO has also developed a scientific early warning system which enables it to detect signs of approaching drought and other weather conditions that can affect farming. The system is used to monitor food and crop outlooks, to warn against developing food shortages, and to assess possible emergency food needs so that preparations for aid are timely. The EROS satellite system, based at Sioux Falls, South Dakota, contributes to the success of FAO's early warning system by photographing the developing stages of droughts and crop conditions.

The FAO has some of its top people working on the issues associated with genetically engineered crops. Organized by the FAO, 150 countries sent delegates to Leipzig, Germany, in 1999 to examine the matter.

Jacques Diouf, a distinguished food and agriculture expert from Senegal, is the director general of the FAO. He was recently elected overwhelmingly to a second six-year term. The FAO has a modest budget of $325 million annually, of which the United States supplies 25 percent, or $81 million. The organization has 3,016 employees, of whom 1,100 are professionals; Americans hold 129 of these professional slots, or 12.5 percent.

THE NEWEST OF the three UN agencies fighting world hunger is the International Fund for Agricultural Development. Founded in 1977, IFAD provides low-interest loans for agricultural and rural development projects. Among international banks and other financial institutions, IFAD's mission is unique: to make loans for rural development projects that will raise nutritional and living standards among the poorest people in the developing countries. This bank uniquely concentrates on loans for the people at the bottom of the economy. Frequently, IFAD will provide grants for FAO-sponsored technical or research activities designed to help farmers or rural communities. IFAD also works with the World Food Program, for example, by including food aid and food-for-work resources from the World Food Program in IFAD-sponsored projects.

One of the IFAD projects that has especially impressed me is the Tamil Nadu Women's Development Project in India. Launched in 1989, the project is devoted to raising the economic and social status of rural women. It makes low-interest loans and training available to women to develop income-producing enterprises such as small-scale cottage industries, including baking, sewing, running food stands, and providing basic health care. The project has targeted the poorest of the poor among rural women, with preference given to female-headed households.

One of the biggest hurdles in the project was the reluctance of local banks to provide credit. But it became clear to Indian bankers that the women's repayment record was excellent, and they have since granted 68,800 loans at a profitable interest rate (12 percent). The project is said to have markedly lifted women's self-confidence and self-esteem and given them the initiative to succeed in small business enterprises.

I saw IFAD projects in Egypt's Nile River valley that are clearly raising the income and productivity of Egyptian farmers. Improved agricultural practices including irrigation are readily apparent. Also, low-cost housing for farmers and villagers is made possible by IFAD low-interest loans.

Visitors to Peru will see a different range of agricultural improvements made possible by IFAD. Projects are focused on peasant families in the poorest rural communities. It is estimated, on the basis of early results, that IFAD's Peruvian projects will increase farm income by 64 percent.

IFAD is funded voluntarily by the member states, which include nearly all the countries of the world. It is a carefully managed fund that makes available loans of about $450 million annually. IFAD operates under the direction of its president, Fauzi H. Al-Sultan, a man well-versed in both banking and agriculture. As is the case with the FAO, the number two post at IFAD is held by an American, the highly regarded John Westly.

These three UN agencies—the World Food Program (WFP), the Food and Agriculture Organization (FAO), and the International Fund for Agricultural Development (IFAD), all based in Rome—are the three institutions to which I have been accredited as U.S. ambassador since 1998. They are supplemented in significant ways by other multilateral agencies, including the World Bank, the International Monetary Fund, the UN Development Program, the World Health Organization, and UNICEF. Also important are the national aid programs, including the U.S. Agency for International Development. Finally, a dedicated, experienced group of religious and philanthropic organizations do marvelous work in bringing food and other necessities to the poor and hungry in all parts of the world.

As I reflect on the dedicated people who reach out to the hungry and the tillers of the soil in the far reaches of the globe, I think of two observations that came to my notice several decades ago. The late American ambassador to India, Chester Bowles, wrote in his *Ambassador's Report:* "I have come to believe that the key to an understanding of Asian villagers is a special reverent concept of land as the source of all wealth and goodness, which those who till the land on every continent seem to have in common."

And then the words of Dwight D. Eisenhower, five-star general and President of the United States: "The peace we seek, founded upon decent trust and cooperative effort among nations, can be fortified, not by weapons of war, but by wheat and cotton; by milk and wool, by meat and by timber and by rice. These are words that translate into every language on earth."

Ofttimes I have pondered the words of our most experienced and respected wartime leaders and have wondered why they are frequently the first among us to warn of the limitations of military power in resolving humanity's ills. Conversely, those most removed from the experience of battle are sometimes the first to advocate the sword, the gun, or the bomb as the instrument of our salvation.

I prefer the views of Bowles and Eisenhower as the proper path to freedom from hunger.

The day I flew my thirty-fifth and final bombing mission over Europe, I brought my bomber back with the fuselage riddled from stem to stern by anti-aircraft fire. That was the day the war in the European theater ended. It was a night of rejoicing: rejoicing that the most destructive war in all history had ended—at least in Europe; rejoicing that we had survived a long string of missions over the most heavily defended targets imaginable; rejoicing that we would soon be flying back home to our beloved USA.

But before we went home our commanding officer, General Nathan Twining, ordered the 15th Air Force to fly an imaginative and compassionate series of peacetime missions. We were instructed to load our bombers with military food rations and fly them into the food-starved areas of war-torn Europe. We would continue to fly these postwar missions until all of our food supplies were gone.

Instead of dropping bombs in Europe, we were now distributing nutritious food. In some instances American food went to hungry Germans who a few days earlier had been trying their best to shoot us out of the skies. I will wager that no European who was fed by this first American airlift after the war will ever forget it. I am even more certain that my fellow pilots and our crews will not forget the pride we felt in converting our bombers to angels of mercy at a terrible time in the life of the world.

This was the spirit that later shaped the great Marshall Plan, Food for Peace, the Peace Corps, America's ongoing foreign assistance, the United Nations, and the religious and philanthropic outreach of the American people. Americans have saved the lives of countless human beings since World War II. And now we will play our part in reaching the 800 million who still hunger and thirst. If those of us who endured the Great Depression and World War II are "the greatest generation," as we have been saluted by Tom Brokaw, then we, with the help of our younger compatriots, will not rest until we win the greatest war of all—the war to achieve freedom from want.

CHAPTER 3

HUNGER: U.S.A.

IN THE SUMMER of 1968, CBS television broadcast a powerful hour-long network documentary, entitled *Hunger: U.S.A.* The cameras had peered into pockets of hunger and misery that were beyond my imagination. Twenty-five million Americans were suffering from hunger and malnutrition, the TV commentator said. There were revealing, heartrending scenes of hungry children, men, and women in the slums of our cities. Hollow cheeks and rickety legs plagued children and adults alike in the rural and mining backwaters of the nation.

But the scene that especially moved me was filmed in a school that required all the students to go to the cafeteria at lunchtime, including those unable to eat because they didn't have the money to pay for lunch. The federal school lunch program had been operating since 1946, but as recently as 1968, it did not provide lunches to the poorest children, who could not pay the modest charge. The cameraman focused on a little boy of nine or ten who was standing at the rear of the room watching the other children eat. "What do you think standing here while your classmates are eating?" asked the TV reporter. Lowering his head and looking at the floor, the boy replied softly, "I'm ashamed." "Why are you ashamed?" the reporter asked. "Because," said the boy, "I ain't got no money."

That night, sitting in my comfortable home in northwest Washington with my wife and children nearby, I, too, was ashamed. I was ashamed because I hadn't known more about hunger in my own land. I was ashamed that a federal program I was supposed to know all about permitted youngsters to go hungry even as they watched paying classmates eat before their eyes.

It was not that little boy who should feel ashamed, I thought. It was I, a U.S. senator living in comfort, who should feel ashamed that there were hungry people—young and old—in my own beloved country.

My country 'tis of thee
Sweet land of liberty.

But what about the 25 million Americans, my fellow citizens, not yet liberated from the bonds of malnutrition? What had I really done, as a U.S. senator, to set free those held captive by the tyranny of hunger?

I retired that night with these questions preying on my mind. When I awakened early the next morning, I knew what I must do: go to the U.S. Senate and introduce a resolution to create a special committee to look into all aspects of the problem of hunger in the United States. My much admired Senate aide, Ben Stong, drafted a Senate resolution and I was able to gain its approval. That action created the Select Committee on Nutrition and Human Needs. Named chairman of the new committee upon its creation, July 30, 1968, I served for nearly a decade, until it was merged with the permanent Senate Committee on Agriculture, December 31, 1977. The combined committee was then renamed the Committee on Agriculture, Nutrition, and Forestry. I served as chairman of the Subcommittee on Nutrition until I left the Senate in 1981.

The Select Committee on Nutrition was one of the great success stories in the history of the Senate. A total of twenty-six senators served on it for varying lengths of time, including Bob Dole, Edward Kennedy, Charles Percy, Allen Ellender, Hubert Humphrey, Jacob Javits, Walter Mondale, Robert Taft, Jr., Herman Talmadge, Gaylord Nelson, and Richard Schweiker.

Senator Dole was crucial to the success of our committee. He joined me in a bipartisan front that became the envy of our colleagues in the Congress. For nearly a decade we pushed through Congress a series of agricultural and nutritional statutes that transformed food and farm assistance in America.

From beginning to end, the committee functioned in a nonpartisan manner. This enabled us to work cooperatively with each other and with the administrations of Presidents Nixon, Ford, and Carter. When the committee's work was completed at the end of 1977, the editors of the *New York Times* credited us with having "led in the war against hunger among the Nation's young, old and poor."

If that editorial judgment was correct, and I am convinced that it was, what was the secret of our success? Several factors were involved.

First, every senator serving on the committee had requested that assignment. Each brought to his work a genuine concern about hunger in America and the desire to do something about it. I cannot recall one incident of partisanship, personal grandstanding, or demagoguery of any kind. All of this enabled us to work productively for the public good.

Second, we had an excellent professional staff. These were the people who planned our public hearings in Washington, supplying superb witnesses. They also set up our field hearings and investigations across the nation. Finally, they wrote our committee reports and made them available to television, radio, newspapers and magazines. We enjoyed an excellent relationship with the press from beginning to end, and this was important to the committee's success in telling our story to the American people.

Third, we capitalized on dramatic insights that fired up the committee and the press. I think of one incident when the newly elected Senator Fritz Hollings, the former governor of South Carolina, was testifying before us in Washington. He said something like the following: I'm from South Carolina and all my life I've been hearing about dumb black people. I used to wonder about that. But now I know, racial epithets aside, it's true. It's true because many of the black people of my state don't have enough to eat and this warps their minds even as it weakens their bodies.

Senator Hollings was right: when undernourished young mothers gave birth to already damaged babies that they were unable to nurse, the result was children whom people refer to as dumb. Mental retardation, or "slow learning," is frequently the byproduct of malnourishment among children and their poorly fed mothers. Along with mothers' alcohol addiction and use of illegal drugs, malnutrition is a major factor in damaging children's intellects.

The committee conducted hearings and investigations in the migrant labor areas of Florida and California, the city slums of the East Coast, the nation's scattered mining towns, and the rural South. Every one of those hearings produced new information and new insights concerning hunger in America.

Hunger: U.S.A.

From the very beginning, our hearings and field investigations were well reported. Members of the media—television, radio, and the press—were always professional. But a constructive, warm, and sometimes humorous relationship developed between the journalists and the senators.

Senator Allen Ellender of Louisiana, a respected, tough-minded older member of our committee, had visited the Soviet Union several times over the years. He wrote a rather lengthy report of his last visit, arguing that the Russian people and their leaders did not want war with the United States and that we should approach them in a more constructive way to achieve better relations. But during our committee's hearings on hunger in the southern part of the United States, he questioned sharply witnesses testifying about the need to expand the food assistance programs in the United States. This prompted the veteran TV reporter Dan Schorr to ask him: "Senator, why are you so soft on Russians, and so hard on Americans?" Dan had a smile on his face, which enabled Ellender to smile, too, but both of them knew that the question made a serious point.

One night while I was having dinner at a hotel dining room during a committee field investigation in Florida, a waiter handed me a note "from a man in the hotel lobby." The note read: "McGovern, you're the guy who wants to take our tax dollars and use them to feed people who are too lazy to work. Take your Committee out of our State and go back to Washington."

I was dead tired after conducting hearings and traveling from one site to another all day long. The note was similar to the message we had heard from the then governor of Florida. I bit my tongue to keep from an angry retort to the governor, but I decided to rebuke the writer of the note by asking him how he could go into the dining room while children in his state were crying from hunger and then attack those who were trying to do something about the problem. I went after the waiter and asked him to point out the man who had written "this outrageous note." When we got to the lobby, he pointed to a man who turned out to be my friend, and a colleague on the committee: Senator Walter Mondale. A great laugh followed and my fatigue vanished.

Some of the highlights of the committee's achievements include:

(1) The food stamp program was reaching fewer than 3 million people when we began work in 1968. A decade later, when our committee was phased out, there were 17 million food stamp recipients. Obviously, this program cost considerable money, but by improving the diet, health, productivity, and learning abilities of millions of children and their families, food stamps probably contributed far more to the educational, economic, and social strength of the nation than anyone could estimate. The stamps are issued monthly to needy families and individuals. They can be used at any grocery store for the purchase of food.

(2) In 1970, Senator Dole and I sponsored changes to the federal school lunch program. Now it would provide a free or reduced-price lunch for low-income students who previously had been unable to participate. This change ended any repetition of the painful scene I had witnessed on television of the little boy embarrassed because he had no money for lunch. Largely because of our committee's efforts, the school lunch program was greatly expanded: 27 million children now participate in it every day. Of these, 12 million receive free or reduced-price lunches.

(3) The summer feeding program for children served 100,000 when our committee was launched. Through our

efforts that number was expanded to 2.5 million youngsters by 1977 and remains at that level.

(4) The school breakfast program grew from 330,000 in 1968 to 2.5 million in 1977 and has held at that level. Most of these breakfasts (2.1 million of them) were free and were given largely to poor children who cannot get a nutritious breakfast at home. School attendance, academic ability, and athletic performance all improved among students who began the day with the nutritious school breakfast. It would be a profitable investment in America's future strength if we offered our students both breakfast and lunch, charging those students who can afford to pay part or all of the cost.

(5) The WIC program, established in the early 1970s, was and remains one of our committee's proudest achievements. A million mothers and infants were participating by 1977. This imaginative program provides nutritious food and counseling to low-income pregnant and nursing mothers and their infants. Social workers, doctors, nurses, and nutritionists all testify to the remarkable success WIC has enjoyed in dramatically improving the health and well-being of millions of mothers and their infants and children below the age of five.

(6) In considerable part, the widespread publicity our Select Committee on Nutrition gained in educating the nation as to the importance of nutrition prompted the Department of Agriculture to establish a Special Mission on Nutrition in 1977. Since then, the department has become a forceful advocate of the whole range of U.S. feeding programs. Nutritional programs, including food stamps, school lunches and WIC, now make up over half of the department's entire budget. Periodically, the USDA also publishes nutritional guidelines that build upon updated versions of our Select Committee's report. The U.S. Department of

Health and Human Services has joined the USDA in this nutritional effort. These two departments have declared that in the year 2000 obesity is the number one nutritional problem in the United States—an ironic conclusion to include in a book on hunger.

(7) In 1977, as a result of the committee's repeated calls, the Congress enacted the first national nutrition education program. Allocating 50 cents per student per year, it created a system of grants to state educational agencies to instruct children on dietary health.

(8) Perhaps the furthest reaching and longest lasting of the committee's achievements was its drafting of the publication *Dietary Goals for the United States.* Since its release in 1977, this report has become a benchmark of the most dependable knowledge about the state of the American diet and what constitutes a healthful diet.

Another report issued by the committee after extensive hearings was *Diet Related to Killer Diseases.* We had learned that six of the ten leading causes of death, including strokes and heart attacks, are related to diet.

With medical care costs skyrocketing and 40 million Americans lacking any health insurance, it is imperative that we devote more time and effort to preventing disease. Sound nutrition is one powerful tool of prevention and good health. Our health system is currently out of balance, with too much being spent after we get sick and not enough on trying to stay healthy. The ten-year work of the Senate Select Committee on Nutrition contributed much to correcting the imbalance between curative and preventive medicine. If all Americans followed a commonsense pattern of eating based on sound nutrition as outlined by the Senate committee, our citizens would be healthier and our medical bills would be lower. With annual medical care costs in the United States pushing past $200 billion in the 1970s, the committee felt this was an additional reason to press for more emphasis on preventive health care, the most important part of which may be good nutrition.

If I could summarize in one sentence the accomplishments of this Senate body, I would say that it laid the foundation of a scientifically and humanely sound nutrition policy for the American people. Second only to my role in forcing an end to the disastrous folly in Vietnam, I would rate my service in leading this work on malnutrition in America as my proudest achievement in the Senate. I continue to mourn the deaths of so many brave young soldiers who died on both sides in a war we never should have fought. I rejoice, however, over the millions of Americans whose lives have been enriched by the Select Committee on Nutrition and Human Needs.

The decade-long record of victories by the Nutrition Committee was made possible by its bipartisan spirit. Senator Dole as the ranking Republican and I as the chairman cooperated closely in planning schedules, hearings, research, and reports followed up with solid legislative achievements on the Senate floor. Those legislative measures were signed into law by Presidents Richard Nixon, Gerald Ford, and Jimmy Carter: two Republicans and one Democrat. They are still the law of the land, and members of both major parties point to that legislation with pride.

I regret to say that in the 1980s, during the administration of Ronald Reagan, the food stamp program was reduced, eliminating several million families from coverage. Other families suffered a reduction of benefits with the termination in the 1990s, during the Clinton administration, of the long-standing Aid to Families with Dependent Children. Largely as a consequence of these two measures, it is now estimated that 31 million Americans do not have enough to eat. Many families exhaust their food stamps before the end of each month, so that for a week or more they don't have adequate food.

These conditions are unacceptable in the United States. We have just completed a decade of unbroken prosperity—admittedly concentrated among the highest-income 20 percent of our citizens, which makes it all the more objectionable that many in the lowest-income 20 percent are hurting. Fortunately, we have low unemployment and low inflation. We have a booming stock market. And we have a balanced budget with a surplus.

We have the food programs in place to end hunger in America right now. We need to expand these programs—especially food stamps—to reach the needy 31 million Americans not now covered. An alternative method to end hunger in America would be to raise the minimum wage; we would then need a smaller expansion of the food stamp program to cover those who don't have jobs. I believe strongly that the international community can end world hunger in our time. But we Americans will feel better about joining in that great effort if we first move quickly to end hunger in our own land.

ONE OF THE TRULY great nongovernmental organizations combating hunger at home and abroad is the Bread for the World Institute, headquartered in Silver Spring, Maryland. Hungry people have no more dedicated and effective advocates than the president of this organization, David Beckman, and its president emeritus, Arthur Simon. Two of their recent publications, *Grace at the Table* and *A*

Hunger: U.S.A.

Program to End Hunger, are essential, compassionate road maps to a world free from hunger. Bread for the World's directors believe that the best way to end hunger in America is twofold: an updating of the food stamp program and a modest raise in the minimum wage. I share that view. We can do no less for those Americans, including millions of children, who do not have enough to eat.

When I watch throngs of people lined up eagerly waiting to be fed within the shadow of the nation's Capitol and the majestic monuments to Washington, Jefferson, and Lincoln, I am once again ashamed. You and I can put an end to that hunger at very little cost to ourselves and with the inner peace that comes with doing what is right. Raising the minimum wage would not cost taxpayers anything; that cost would be borne by all of us as consumers. A tax cost of approximately $3 billion, or about $30 for each taxpayer, would expand the food stamp program to reach those who still need it.

It is one of the cruel paradoxes of our time that the world's richest nation still has millions of hungry citizens. According to a recent congressional study, approximately one-ninth of Americans are hungry simply because they can't afford food for themselves and their families for at least some part of each month. Twelve million of these hungry— about 40 percent—are children. If our government could decisively address hunger during the scarcity times of the 1930s, surely we can do at least as well in today's affluent times.

Since 1985, food assistance to the poor has been cut back substantially. Poor families usually receive $100 to $200 monthly in food stamps to safeguard them from malnutrition; it is estimated that nearly four-fifths of recipients run out of stamps before the end of the month. Our government has exhorted the churches to help make up for the federal reductions with increased charitable efforts. However, to fully compensate for cutbacks in government food programs, every one of the country's 350,000 churches would have to contribute an average of $150,000 in food every year—more than the annual budgets of the vast majority of them.

This is the first time in American history that hunger and poverty have not significantly diminished during a sustained period of economic growth. The problem is that most of this new wealth has gone to the wealthiest Americans. While unemployment is low, many jobs do not pay a wage adequate to feed a family. Indeed, the degree of income disparity in America—the gap between the rich and the poor—is the largest in any Western industrialized nation and is comparable to that of many Third World countries.

Welfare recipients are now required to find work, often at the minimum wage or if they are lucky at $6, $7, or $8 an hour, yet they do not have adequate support for child care or health insurance. Indeed, the odds of a welfare mother finding a job that pays a living wage are very slim. Nearly half of the nation's hungry families include at least one member who works full-time. Meanwhile, the decline in decently paid, unionized industrial jobs, the cutbacks in health care and other benefits, and the runaway shops seeking cheaper labor overseas have set an unprecedented number of American families scrambling for food even at a time of national prosperity.

The Universal Declaration of Human Rights, now more than fifty years old, recognizes the right to food. But the United States has refused to ratify the International Covenant for Economic, Social and Cultural Rights, which codifies many of the basic human rights articulated in the declaration, including the right to food. The United States is the only member of the G-8, the group of leading industrialized democracies, which has not ratified the Covenant. We are also the only industrial nation that permits millions of its poor to go without adequate food.

Many Americans are unaware of the level of hunger and malnutrition in our country. It is not a topic the media tend to cover. Most middle-class and wealthy Americans consciously avoid going into poor urban and rural areas, so they fail to see the stark reality of undernourished people in their own country. Right-wing think tanks, funded by corporate interests and wealthy conservatives, as well as by their allies in the media, have played a major role in distorting the reality of poverty in America and the role of government in alleviating it. An election night poll in 1994 showed that most voters thought that either welfare or foreign aid was the largest item in the federal budget. In reality, together they make up less than 3 percent, a tiny fraction of the 18 percent of the budget accounted for by military spending.

Even some of those who support federal programs to help hungry Americans take politicians' professions of concern for the poor at face value, failing to notice how little is actually being done. A classic case is that of President Richard Nixon, who hosted a White House Conference on Food, Nutrition and Health at which he stated, "The moment is at hand to put an end to hunger in America"; privately, he told his secretary of agriculture to "use all the rhetoric so long as it doesn't cost money." (I must add, however, that President Nixon always signed without complaint the nutritional measures authored by Senator Dole and me.)

Despite some insensitivity toward America's hungry by political leaders and the mainstream media, and despite the badly distorted public understanding of the problem and the government's role, public support for government's obligation to the poor is as strong as ever. According to a 1998 public opinion poll by the Pew Research Center for the People and the Press, 72 percent of Americans believe that government "should see to it that no one is without food, clothing and shelter." This is as high as when President Lyndon Johnson was launching the Great Society programs in 1965 and when I was the Democratic nominee for president in 1972. The same proportion of Americans has told pollsters that ending world hunger should be the top priority of American foreign policy.

Indeed, cutbacks over the past two decades in programs supporting poor and hungry Americans would have been far more severe were it not for popular mobilizations by antihunger groups and advocates for the poor to defend these modest government efforts and the clear, widespread support for their continuation.

We pay a price for this domestic hunger, in health care for those who come down with diseases that cost a lot of money to treat but could have been avoided with adequate nutrition, and for keeping alive babies with low birthweights caused by their mothers' undernourishment. We pay the price in children who drop out of school because they are too malnourished to concentrate, only to find a life on the streets and in criminal activity. There is no excuse not to make a decisive effort to end hunger in America, both for the sake of the poor and for everyone else.

CHAPTER 4

WOMEN AND GIRLS

THE MOST VALUABLE investment that can be made in the Third World is to improve the education of girls. This is McGovern's Law Number One for advancing the countries of the developing world. As matters now stand, there are an estimated 565 million illiterate women around the world, mostly in poor rural regions of the developing countries. Imagine the loss to our global community that comes from this blanket of ignorance. Despite the fact that many Third World governments and outside assistance groups know the necessity of educating girls as well as boys, 73 million girls of primary school age are not in school. Looking at this shocking fact, the International Food Policy Research Institute, a nonprofit group located in Washington, D.C., says bluntly that "if the world is to make a sizable dent in poverty and hunger in the next two decades, getting these girls into school will clearly have to be part of the equation." I have no doubt about that. In 1992, Lawrence Summers, then vice president and chief economist of the World Bank and now U.S. Secretary of the Treasury, concluded: "When one takes into account all its benefits, educating girls yields a higher rate of return than any other investment available in the developing world."

If the international community will resolve to invest its influence and resources in improving the educational, medical, economic, and political opportunities for girls, that will do more to reduce world hunger and help the developing countries than any other single step.

Why is this true? It is true first of all because girls make up half of the youthful population of the Third World; and at present, with few exceptions, the members of that half of young humanity are functioning far below their potential capacities because of favoritism toward boys and discrimination against girls.

This is true, for instance, in the all-important realm of education. Boys in the developing countries are pushed forward toward higher education while girls are encouraged instead to amass a dowry, get married, and start having children—many of them before they have even reached their teenage years. Having more children at the youngest possible age is not what Africa, Asia, and Latin America most need from their girls. What is most needed are better-educated girls equipped to care intelligently for the children who are already here—as well as for those yet to come. Girls between the ages of eleven and eighteen should be in school, not in the marriage bed. And if some of them can go on to college before they marry, so much the better.

Experience has repeatedly demonstrated that when girls are educated, they marry later and have fewer children. That would not be unwelcome in our overcrowded world.

A recent study in Mexico demonstrated that the education of girls was the most important single factor in reducing the birthrate and in improving the care and health of infants. Many women interviewed for this study said that education had given them the opportunity for jobs and a measure of economic independence. Others simply observed that education had given them a better and happier life. Women were quick to say that education had lifted their social standing and enabled them to defend themselves and care for their children if they were deserted by their husbands or their marriages failed.

One woman told World Food Program researchers that without schooling, "I didn't know anything." Imagine this woman as a little girl—doubtless with an ignorant, uneducated mother—growing up without education, only to reach the demoralized state of realizing as an adult that she "didn't know anything." Then she added: "If I had a daughter, I would say it would be better for her to study so she wouldn't be the same as I was."

Some students of global hunger believe that there must be a reduction in the birthrate if the food producers of the world are to catch up with the growing number of hungry stomachs. To whatever extent that is true, the most important way to cut birthrates is to educate girls. Extending the education of boys has no measurable effect on fertility rates, but a recent World Bank study demonstrates that for each additional year of education girls receive, the birthrate in that community goes down by as much as 10 percent.

Another study, run in Zimbabwe by the Cambridge Female Education Trust, found that of 387 girls who completed high school, only 5 percent became mothers between the ages of eighteen and twenty-four, whereas in the nation as a whole, 47 percent of girls in that age bracket gave birth to one or more children. Many of these girls had little or no education, and a high percentage of them had children in their teens. "The value of education is so strong that girls do want to continue it if they are given the chance. Moreover, they want to secure their economic situation before starting a family," the Cambridge study concluded. There are now seventy-nine businesses run by educated young women in Zimbabwe—still only a small fraction of the total, but a significant beginning.

In the Philippines, a comparative study of boys and girls produced interesting results. Boys on the average inherited .19 hectares of land more than girls. Girls, on the other hand, stayed in school 1.5 years more than boys—a reversal of the usual pattern, where favoritism toward boys includes more years in school. In this competition between land and education, the lifetime income of girls ranged from 10 to 100 percent higher than that of the boys.

The authors of still another World Bank study concluded that giving girls a better education creates a decidedly better environment for national economic growth. This is true because instead of being a drag on the community's development, young women who are educated can join in the development process. It is interesting to note that as girls rise educationally, they are taken more seriously by males and by the community.

Perhaps most impressively, there is clear evidence that educated girls pass on the benefits of their education to their children. A study in 1998 by a respected nutrition group known as 2020 Vision, found that in sixty-three Third World countries, the education of mothers was "by far the most important reason why child malnutrition decreased by 15.5 percent between 1970 and 1995—much more important than, for instance, improved health environments or food availability."

Again, Lawrence Haddad, a nutritional expert writing for 2020 Vision, asserts: "Partly because a mother uses her new knowledge and the additional income she earns from it to improve diets, care, and sanitation for her children, female education is probably the strongest instrument we have for

reducing infant mortality and child malnutrition." In support of this conclusion, the World Development Report
noted that a 10 percent increase in female literacy reduced
child deaths by an equal proportion in thirteen African
countries between 1975 and 1985. In Peru during the
1980s, even four to six years of schooling for girls reduced
the risk of infant deaths by 40 percent; seven or more years
reduced deaths by 75 percent.

And then this final note, from John Hoddinott of the International Food Policy Research Institute: "Children of
educated mothers do better in school because children are
healthier, mothers can help them with their homework, educated mothers can be role models, especially for girls, and
mothers may be less intimidated by their children's teachers
(or by their children!)."

An educated mother is perhaps society's most precious
asset. Until a child begins school at the age of five or six, the
most important educational and cultural influence is its
mother. An ignorant mother can unwittingly retard her
child's future educational development. Conversely, an educated mother can be an important, mind-opening inspira-
tion to the child.

I have noted in recent years that when American athletic
stars, especially African Americans, are interviewed on television about their athletic brilliance, they will frequently
say, "I owe it all to my mother."

The more we can press for the elevation of the girls of
the developing countries, the more Michael Jordans, Albert
Einsteins, Marie Curies, Nelson Mandelas, and Joan Suther-
lands they might produce.

Every reasonable effort to improve the health, nutrition,
and sanitary habits of girls will also prove a wise investment.
Obviously, the same considerations apply to boys, but given

that girls are potential future mothers, it is especially important that they develop good basic health and nutritional
habits in their own lives and that they apply those habits in
rearing their infants and children. Healthy, educated girls
are treasures in any society.

One of the saddest results of the discrimination against
girls—even infant girls—and women is excess mortality
among women. In Europe, Canada, and the United States,
the life span of women is longer than that of men. Not so
in China, India, and Africa, where the life span of women
is markedly lower than that of the men. The Nobel
Prize–winning economist Amartya Sen points out that if
the female and male life spans were proportionately the
same in China and India as in Europe and the United
States, there would be another 50 million women in
China, and the same number in India. Dr. Sen calls these
100 million the missing women. "The main culprit," he
says in his book *Development as Freedom,* "would seem to be
the comparative neglect of female health and nutrition, especially—but not exclusively—during childhood. There is
indeed considerable direct evidence that female children
are neglected in terms of health care, hospitalization and
even feeding."

Giving birth at a very young age is more medically dangerous than doing so at a more mature age—another threat
to the health and survival of young girls. For children to
have children is not good for either mothers or infants, for a
number of reasons not difficult to imagine.

Health services to girls should include counseling about
and access to the birth control measures so widely used in
the developed world. But there are other fundamental factors to be considered in reducing Third World birthrates, of
which the reduction in poverty may be the most significant.

Women and Girls

Some will contend that poverty is caused by excessive population growth. Obviously, it costs more to sustain eight children than it does two; so many large families fall into poverty partly because of their sheer size. But high fertility rates in poor countries are at least as much a reflection of poverty and inequality as the cause of them. So long as the financial security of the mother is dependent largely on her surviving children, she will agree to have or seek to have more children as her old-age insurance. If an uneducated woman has few or no opportunities for paid jobs, and her power and influence are based on the number of her offspring, especially males, then the birthrate will be high for both social and economic reasons. One definite similarity between developed and developing nations is that the women in both worlds who are educated and have paying jobs have fewer children.

Female children are disproportionately affected by hunger. Twelve million youngsters are now dying annually in the Third World, which is more than the number of people who died annually in the Second World War. Each day 34,000 children die of hunger and related diseases. India has made great increases in grain production since I first visited there in the 1960s, thanks to the Green Revolution, which focused much of its energy on that country. Today, the total number of chronically hungry Indians has been reduced to one-fifth of the population; yet half of the country's preschool children are malnourished, and a majority of the hungry are girls according to the WFP.

Today's poorly fed pregnant or nursing mothers, many of them very young, are producing tomorrow's barriers to personal, social, and economic development—malnourished, brain-dulled, listless children. Those fortunate enough to survive will struggle through uncertain lives, diminished as productive, happy persons. Undernourished children born to undernourished mothers face a greater risk of neurological disorders that threaten their ability to see, hear, and learn. They are more prone to malaria and respiratory diseases; indeed, it is estimated that half of all disease-related mortality among infants around the world could be avoided if these children and their mothers were adequately fed. Eradicating chronic hunger is both a moral imperative and a profitable investment in the future of our planet.

DISCRIMINATION AGAINST GIRLS and women is most prevalent with respect to opportunities for jobs outside the home. Nearly two-thirds of the workforce in the Third World is agricultural. This agricultural labor is the developing world's most valuable resource and the one that most needs to be developed—free from gender or class discrimination.

Perhaps many of us, when we think of the teeming workforce in places like India, China, Russia, Latin America, and Africa, have an image of the male peasant toiling in the hot, sun-drenched fields while his wife is at home coolly rocking the cradle. Nothing could be more mistaken. In Africa, 80 percent of the food consumed in people's homes is produced by women in the gardens and fields. Yet it is the male-dominated cash export crops—cotton, coffee, hemp, grains—that have received nearly all the foreign aid and are now a growing part of the new global trading system.

The same pattern exists in other regions. The women produce the yams, turnips, potatoes, other vegetables, and fruits. They also tend the chickens and eggs, feed the pigs, and work for hours daily in the fields, side by side with their husbands if they have husbands, alone if they do not. Women and girls produce and prepare nearly all of the world's table food, mostly to feed their own families and neighbors.

Eight out of ten working farmers in Africa are women. In Asia, the ratio is six out of ten. Around the globe women are the sole breadwinners in a third of the households. I have noticed far more men than women milling idly around village centers during the heat of the day. Yet, nearly all agricultural credit from banks and corporate conglomerates goes to men, to finance export crops. The banks simply don't believe in loaning money to women. The reason for this may be the uncomfortable fact that despite World Food Program findings that women produce 90 percent of all food consumed in the homes of the Third World, they own only 1 percent of the farmland. If the banks are looking for collateral to secure their loans, whether for farming or for the opening of village shops, where do they find it? Only in the hands of landowning men.

This imbalance is actually worsening: as traditional communal lands become privatized, they tend to go to men, who will use them for cash crops for export. Women are the key to assuring household food security and should be given more consideration in the granting of bank credit, local public assistance, and international aid.

I am pleased to report that the World Food Program is now seeking to give local women a leading role in all the field operations that assist developing societies. WFP does so because a number of studies, especially one in Bangladesh, have clearly documented that when the woman of the family has some control over food and income, the children are better nourished and the entire family does better in nearly every way than when income and food are controlled entirely by the man.

I am encouraged by reports indicating that in addition to the World Food Program, another superb United Nations program, UNICEF, headquartered in New York, is now emphasizing the importance of girls and women in improving living standards in the Third World. It is worth noting that these agencies trying to elevate the status of women and girls are both headed by women—unusually capable and courageous women, both Americans, Catherine Bertini of the World Food Program and Carol Bellamy of UNICEF. Needless to say, many of the men in leadership roles of the UN agencies are also sensitive and caring about gender issues. For example, Ms. Bellamy was preceded by the late Jim Grant, who directed UNICEF for many years—one of the most dedicated and unprejudiced public servants I have known anywhere in the world.

It is uncomfortable to realize that in spite of the fact that they produce most of the world's household food, women and girls make up most of the world's hungry people according to the UN Food and Agriculture Organization. The same studies by the FAO document that seventy percent of the world's illiterate people are females and most of the world's poorest people are girls and women. Even in countries moving toward political democracy, few public offices are held or even aspired to by women.

I don't want to live in this kind of unbalanced world without doing more to set it right. Who in his right mind would want to discriminate against those who bring so much intelligence, grace, beauty, and love to our lives everywhere around the world as do women and girls?

I don't know whether anyone has yet formulated these ideas as laws of development, but I would be proud to claim them as McGovern's Laws: (1) To maximize the benefits of food aid for the entire family, give the food to Mom and the girls. (2) To maximize the benefits of agricultural credit and other farm aid, make sure that women are eligible as well as the men. (3) If capable people are needed to run bakeries, food markets, clothing shops, health clinics, and telephone, radio, and computer services, consider the women and girls as well as the men and boys. (4) If you're distributing loans for higher education, don't forget the half of young people who are girls, every bit as smart and promising as the boys. (5) If qualified candidates or appointees are needed for the town council, the school board, the district assembly, look for quality candidates or appointees among the women as well as the men.

Fortunately, a number of people in a position to help correct the imbalances between males and females are working at that task. Following the Fourth World Conference on Women at Beijing in 1995, the World Food Program adopted its own "commitments to women," as follows:

- 80 percent of food relief will be distributed directly to women;
- 60 percent of WFP's nonfood aid, such as technical assistance and job training, will go to women and girls;
- 50 percent of WFP's educational resources in each country will go to girls.

The World Food Program is determined to achieve these goals by 2001.

These are not simply feminist dreams; they are also well-thought-out conclusions based on experience in the field about how best to get the job done: ending world hunger. The blunt truth is there will be no end to hunger until women and girls are fully enlisted in the battle, as befits their abilities and their rights as dignified, precious human beings.

Catherine Bertini has said repeatedly that the elevation of women is vital to liberating people around the world who are trapped by hunger and poverty. Not content with resolutions and commitments, Bertini has thrown her humanitarian forces into action in some of the toughest places in the world—North Korea, Rwanda, Kosovo, Angola, Bosnia, Vietnam, and now Afghanistan. On some missions of mercy to troubled areas, including one to Rwanda in 1999, her talented, dedicated people have lost their lives.

If there is any one country where life is especially hard and hazardous for girls and women, it is terribly poor, war-devastated Afghanistan. Afghanistan has been blasted and bled over more than twenty years of continuous warfare. Its latest rulers are the Taliban militia, who acquired billions of dollars' worth of lethal American and Saudi arms when our leaders thought supplying such arms was the best way to make life miserable for the Soviet Union.

Moscow saw neighboring Afghanistan as being a part of its zone of influence and sent its forces in to install a more acceptable government. In retrospect, our policymakers were probably mistaken in thwarting the Russian objectives by equipping the Mujahedeen with arms. The Taliban was an extremist, hard-line faction of the Mujahedeen who then fought their way into control of the country. In hindsight it is hard to imagine a Russian-supported government worse than the Taliban with their deadly modern American weapons.

Women and Girls

In November 1995, at the urging of the United States, the UN applied economic sanctions against the Taliban because of their refusal to expel the notorious terrorist Osama bin Laden.

The Taliban are an aggressive, ruthless band that clings to an obvious distortion of the Muslim faith. They are especially oppressive toward women. They require that girls and women be covered in black from the tops of their heads to the soles of their feet. The slightest deviation brings a public whipping and a possible jail term. Girls are prevented from going to school; for good measure, popular music and television are banned for everybody, male and female. Both girls and women are forbidden to work outside the home. Since an estimated 70 percent of the residents of Kabul, the nation's capital, are unemployed, jobs are scarce for men also. Half of all the buildings in the city have been destroyed by warfare, and there are no funds or materials to rebuild them. Kabul has a population of 1.6 million. Every day 400,000 of them line up to receive bread or wheat from the UN, the Red Cross, and other charitable organizations. No other food except possibly a little weak tea or a spoiled apple is available.

In 1996 a UN-conducted survey of Afghanistan revealed the following conditions: more than one child in four died before reaching the age of five; life expectancy was forty-four years; illiteracy was 30 percent. Hunger and malnutrition among children and the general populace were the rule rather than the exception. Some of those conditions, including the shortages of housing and food, have gotten worse.

Notwithstanding the Taliban's repressive grip on Afghan females, Bertini and her deputies discovered a way around the ban on females working outside the home. WFP now supplies flour to thirty-seven bakeries where only girls and women are permitted to work (to avoid exposure to lustful men in the workplace). Furthermore, the bakeries sell their bread—the country's traditional flat bread—only to women and children, so there is no potentially sinful contact with men here. Eventually WFP will hand over the bakeries to their women employees so they can be run as independent, income-producing enterprises. The bakeries have markedly enhanced the income, power, and independence of women, and have taught them business methods and decision-making.

When the World Food Program arrived in Angola in 1997, it not only brought food to hungry people, but also attacked the problem of abused girls. Civil conflict has disrupted their homes and families. On the streets of Luanda, the capital of Angola—another war-torn country—girls as young as eight, nine, and ten are routinely raped or forced to yield their bodies to older men to get a few coins for a meal. It is estimated that more than a thousand young girls are sexually abused every day by strangers, irresponsible guardians, and even some local government authorities, police, and soldiers.

In a short time WFP used some of its food aid as wages to pay people for rehabilitating a big old house in central Luanda. It then brought in from the streets a hundred of the most seriously abused girls between the ages of eight and twelve. WFP gives each girl not only a comfortable bed in a spacious home, but also daily food rations and training in household skills and personal health. Fifty additional girls, for whom there is no room in the home, come each day for a nutritious hot meal and for the training courses.

Julia Vasconcelos, the WFP officer in Luanda, observed recently: "These girls have been the victims of serious violence, and they have a lot of anger in them. We want to help them, to work with them until they are old enough to get education and jobs through government ministries for women." The ripple impact on Angolan society of "saving" perhaps 150 formative-age girls is immeasurable. When they "graduate," they will be replaced by other girls needing rehabilitation and healing, who will then also be better equipped to face the hard life of Angola.

The World Food Program has also reached out to girls in numerous other countries. In two tiny places seldom in the news, Benin and Niger, WFP devised a food program under which girls were not only fed at school, but were also sent home with food rations for their families. When this program was introduced in the schools of Benin, the number of girls in school shot up 280 percent. Ninety-two percent of them remained in school; and having eaten their school lunches, they faithfully took the family rations home. The overall performance of both the girls and their families improved measurably. In Niger, where only 19 percent of eligible-age girls were attending primary school and 93 percent of the women were illiterate, the results were similar to the experience in Benin.

One of the world's poorest countries is Bangladesh. My wife, Eleanor, and I were there on New Year's Day, 1976, en route to a Senate Foreign Relations Committee mission to Vietnam. While there, we were dinner guests at the tidy but very modest home of the young foreign minister. Each person was given a small serving of grated, uncooked cabbage on one side of the plate and on the other a single hard-boiled egg. After thanking me for my efforts to end the killing in Vietnam, the minister and his wife smiled wistfully in the knowledge that they had been able to secure an egg for each of the six people at the table. With Bangladesh's annual per capita income at less than $100, not many people had enough money to buy six eggs and give them away to visitors. I had the nervous feeling that I was eating an egg that should have gone to the minister's four children.

But in Bangladesh today the World Food Program is using its resources especially to help girls and women. WFP surveyed the situation there and decided that women and girls needed an on-the-job training program in which food could be used as wages. More than 1.5 million women and girls were trained for jobs under this program. Altogether more than 8 million women and children have participated in feeding programs. Two years after the food-for-wages job training program was completed, dramatic results were documented. Earnings in the households of participants were substantially higher and still rising; household food consumption was up, as were nutritional standards; housing was improved; and household financial assets had grown. Many of the girls and women involved in sustainable income-producing activities were highly pleased that they had increased their social status, their independence, their mobility, and their control over money and other resources. Partly because of the newly released energy and creativity of these women and girls, the per capita income of Bangladesh has tripled since I was there in 1976.

The kind of well-conceived interventions just described plus rapid responses to natural disasters and violence have made the World Food Program the largest food assistance agency in the world. It needs to be even larger if we are to win the battle against hunger. Embattled armies around the world fire off shells in one day that cost more than the entire annual budget of the World Food Program. Destruction has always cost more than prevention and healing. As an American, I am especially proud of two facts about the World Food Program: the United States donates the lion's share of the WFP budget; and the agency is working hard to see that girls born in the Third World have the same opportunities for food, schooling, health, and jobs as boys.

The largest agency in the world trying to improve agriculture and the production of food is the UN Food and Agriculture Organization, which frequently cooperates with WFP and the International Fund for Agricultural Development (essentially a farmers' bank). FAO and IFAD, like WFP, are located in Rome. The three agencies coordinate activities when practical, and all three are working to address the neglected problems of women and girls.

Following the 1995 UN Conference on Women in Beijing, the FAO drew up its "Plan of Action for Women in Development (1996-2001)." Dr. Diouf, a champion of women's rights, introduced the plan with these words: "Women continue to provide food for their families despite limited access to land, credit, capital and technology, lack of education, training and information, and an unfavorable legal and policy environment. The perseverance with which rural women confront these obstacles signals the vast untapped potential that could be released to benefit both this generation and future generations."

There it is—Dr. Diouf, a distinguished food and agriculture scientist whose home is Senegal in West Africa—makes the case eloquently for emancipating the patient, long-suffering girls and women of much of the Third World.

If we can find ways of persuading our Third World brothers to undo the bonds now blocking the potential contributions of their girls and women, we can end hunger in our time. If those bonds are not loosened, then world hunger will linger on, taking its terrible toll on men and women, boys and girls, for generations to come.

CHAPTER 5

THE VICIOUS CIRCLE: HUNGER, CONFLICT, MORE HUNGER

IN THE PREVIOUS CHAPTER I contended that we can't overcome world hunger until the women of the Third World are educated and fully enlisted in the development of their countries. We can't have half the population held back by enforced ignorance, poor health, job discrimination, and other gender inequities and then expect hunger to vanish through some male miracle. No society can afford gender discrimination—especially not where all hands and minds are needed in the development process.

I begin this chapter with two more propositions:

First, world hunger cannot be ended unless the developing countries achieve more responsible governments. This calls for a greater measure of democracy with political and civil rights, and a responsiveness to basic human needs—food security, safe water, health services, and education. It will take some years to reach these goals. Indeed, they are not yet fully achieved even in some of the more developed countries. But they are the objectives toward which every humane and serviceable government should attempt to move. Each step taken on the way is cause for rejoicing among the hungry.

Second, there will be no end to hunger until Third World countries find ways to resolve their nationalistic, ethnic, religious, and tribal conflicts without violence. The terrible slaughters taking place in the developing world—slaughters like those long embraced on a mass scale by the developed countries—have to stop if humanity is to be freed from hunger.

These two propositions are intertwined. Governments that are more responsive to the will and well-being of their people will be less likely to exhaust the resources of the country in destructive conflict, which hurts everyone. Also, governments more sensitive to the needs of the people will be less likely to provoke uprisings that destroy people and resources essential to the struggle against hunger and poverty.

The evidence is clear that responsible, democratic governments are much more likely to lead the way toward food security than are dictatorships indifferent to the public's well-being. Since democratic rulers depend upon the approval and votes of the citizens, they must address the needs of ordinary citizens if they are to remain in power.

Authoritarian or colonial rulers who are themselves not hurt by chronic hunger, famines, or other troubles have no incentive to give time and attention to the need for measures to either reduce ever present hunger or to prevent famines. Such leaders are even less likely to deal systematically with the less extreme but more widespread chronic hunger that afflicts so many Third World societies. Democratic governments, on the other hand, have to live with criticism from the public and, in some cases, from a free press. They also have to face elections, and they know that a famine against which they took no precautions could drive them from office. Sooner or later democratic governments will be called to account by hungry electorates.

Even such poor countries as Botswana, India, and Zimbabwe have not had any widespread famines. The reason, it would seem, is that they have become democratic since winning their independence. At least partially because they knew elections were ahead, the leaders of these countries have taken preventive steps to avoid the ravages of famine. The fear of defeat at the polling place greatly focuses the mind of an incumbent politician. Nonetheless, malnutrition is still widespread in these countries and the populations are stirring restlessly.

Famines have historically hit colonies, such as India and Ireland when they were under British rule; one-party states, such as the Ukraine in the 1930s, China in 1958–1961, and Cambodia in the 1970s; and military dictatorships, such as Ethiopia, Somalia, North Korea, and Sudan.

Consider the Irish famine of the 1840s. I once believed, even as a historian by profession, that this terrible famine was solely the result of the potato blight. But all during this period, when millions of Irish faced starvation and the proportionally largest forced migration in history (mostly to the United States), there was ample food in Britain that could have assisted the Irish. Furthermore, Irish farmers had to sell their cattle, pigs, butter, eggs, wheat, and oats to England to avoid bankruptcy because their countrymen were too impoverished to buy anything. The British were free to ignore the Irish—their colonial subjects—whereas if the danger of famine had arisen in England, the government probably would have quickly responded to counter it. Indeed, as Amartya Sen writes in his great treatise, *Development as Freedom* (p. 175): "Famines are, in fact, so easy to prevent that it is amazing that they are allowed to occur at all."

The British official in charge of economic policy during the "potato" famine, Charles Trevelyan, saw the problem not as a failure of government response, but as a result of the Irish poor eating only potatoes. As he put it: "There is scarcely a woman of the peasant class in the West of Ireland whose culinary art exceeds the boiling of a potato." Dr. Sen's comment on this observation is worth noting: "The remark is of interest not just because it is rather rare for an Englishman to find a suitable occasion for making international criticism of culinary art! Rather, the pointing of an accusing finger at the meagerness of the diet of the Irish poor well illustrates the tendency to blame the victim" (ibid., p. 175).

One sees the same tendency to blame the victim in Winston Churchill, when he said the 1943 famine in the Indian province of Bengal was caused by the tendency of the natives to breed "like rabbits." Perhaps Sir Winston's view of excessive reproduction as the cause of famine was acquired in his school days; he may have misread Jonathan Swift's satirical barb, "A Modest Proposal," aimed at the British ruling class. To those who believed that Ireland's eighteenth-century poverty was caused by an excess of children, Swift suggested sarcastically that they should resolve the problem by purchasing the excess at 10 shillings a head and eating them.

Churchill, the great British World War II leader, having unburdened himself on the matter of Indian reproductive habits, further classified the Indians as "the beastliest people in the world, next to the Germans." Poor Churchill, beset on one hand by beastly Germans trying unsuccessfully to

defeat him in battle, and on the other by beastly Indians trying successfully to win their independence.

It is worth repeating that since Mahatma Gandhi led the
"beastly Indians" to independence and democracy more
than a half-century ago, India has not experienced a single
famine and is now self-sufficient in food. It would appear
that both the breeding habits and the beastly behavior of
the Indians have improved since the Indians broke free of
English rule. The record is most convincing that natural disasters alone seldom, if ever, create famines.

The horrific mid-1980s famine in the African Sahel, the
arid region on the southern flank of the Sahara Desert that
stretches across several countries including Senegal and
Chad, was only indirectly a result of drought. Peasant farmers, in debt to wealthy merchants, were forced to sell their
land and no longer had access to food to sustain themselves,
particularly since many of the merchants hiked prices in response to crop shortfalls. Thus, while production had certainly been reduced by the dry weather, there was still
enough food to have fed the population. It was debt and
high food prices, not drought, that ultimately caused the
famine.

Many famines are often selective or even hidden, affect-
ing a minority of the population, primarily poor women
and children, since families will often consciously or un-
consciously allocate most or all available food to their
working males. Food often is available locally but is unaf-
fordable or is being hoarded. In the past, food aid has sometimes gone to a region without careful evaluation of who
within the affected area most needs the food. Those involved in relief efforts must have the resources not only to
bring food in, but also to distribute it to those who most
need it.

Similarly, most of the recent natural disasters for which the World Food Program and private voluntary organizations provided relief were not simply acts of God. The use of prime agricultural land for plantations of cash crops were what forced peasants in Central America and Venezuela onto steep hillsides vulnerable to landslides, and peasants of the African Sahel into marginal, drought-prone regions. The clear-cutting of forests around the Indian and Nepalese tributaries of the Ganges River contributed greatly to the disastrous floods downstream in Bangladesh. North Korea's rigid totalitarian political and economic system has contributed at least as much to that country's ongoing famine as has the weather. That government has been more interested in maintaining its military power and iron-fisted government than it has in the well-being of ordinary citizens. Wars greatly exacerbated the hunger emergencies resulting from recent droughts in the Horn of Africa and earthquakes in Afghanistan. Indeed, thirty-one African countries were affected by the drought of the early 1980s, but the only ones that actually experienced famine—Angola, Mozambique, Chad, Sudan, and Ethiopia—were in the midst of war. Some of the worst hunger emergencies in recent years— such as in Rwanda, Sudan, Kosovo, Sierra Leone, and Liberia—had nothing to do with nature at all, but were a result of ethnic fighting. Indeed, food emergencies that are a direct consequence of war have risen dramatically. In 1970, a million people received food aid because of armed conflict. Today, that figure stands at more than 20 million. Internal civil and ethnic conflicts have now surpassed war between nations—and every other problem—as the world's primary cause of both famine and chronic hunger.

The strain on food aid resources does not end when the fighting stops. Currently, there are more than 25 million refugees in the world, many of whom—unable to farm or otherwise provide for their families—depend on food aid on an ongoing basis. There are at least that many internally displaced persons, many of whom also depend on food aid. In both cases, the local communities hosting these populations are negatively affected, as well: demands are placed on their resources, commodity prices rise, labor markets are disrupted, and development activities are cut back, all of which threatens the food security of even those not directly involved in the conflict.

It has always troubled me that so many of the weapons used in these devastating conflicts come from the United States. One of the most important steps our government could take in the fight against hunger would be to make a serious effort to curb the international arms trade, beginning with reductions in our own sales. Third World countries can't afford to waste their resources buying these arms and it is in our own long-term interest to stop selling arms all over the developing world. These arms inevitably encourage violent conflict while draining already burdened national treasuries. We should be on the side of reducing poverty and hunger rather than fostering violence.

Unilateral sanctions, such as the U.S. embargo of Cuba and sanctions against Armenia by some of its neighbors, have also contributed to periodic food shortages in these countries. It is ironic, in an era when advocacy of free trade has become almost an article of faith, that, in the face of the recent severe drought in eastern Cuba, our government still considered it a crime for Americans to send food to hungry Cuban children.

Aside from the more visible human failings that have produced famines, there is one not so visible but no less serious concern on the horizon: global warming is contributing to severe droughts and flooding, which, in turn, have created some of the worst food emergencies of the last few years. Global warming does not simply mean an even rise of temperatures, which could conceivably reduce world hunger if it brought a longer growing season in countries such as Canada and Russia. Instead, we will see higher temperatures in some places but colder temperatures elsewhere, greater extremes in temperatures all around, and disrupted weather patterns that result in more severe storms and droughts. It is widely recognized that global warming contributed to the unusual severity of the most recent episode of the El Niño weather pattern. The world's nations met in Kyoto, Japan, in 1996 to try to tackle this problem, and negotiated a modest treaty to try to control emissions that contribute to global warming. Unfortunately, the United States—the largest contributor to such emissions—has thus far failed to ratify the treaty, and many other nations have delayed ratification in response.

Both the historical record and the expert analyses of respected social scientists leave no doubt that people will be exposed to less danger of famine and starvation if they are subject to popularly elected governments. Needless to say, civil rights and political freedom confer other huge benefits too. Freedom of speech, of religion, and of the press enriches the lives of people culturally, intellectually, and spiritually. Free elections are sometimes flawed, but who, other than dictators and their privileged allies, would want to live in a country without elections? We sometimes get weary of public criticism and heated political debates, but which of us would want to live in a society that did not allow public criticism and debate? Free enterprise sometimes needs a measure of regulation to protect the public from its excesses, as we are now seeing in Russia and as was experienced by the Western industrial countries in an earlier age, but the principle of freedom to own one's business and to farm one's own land is a sound and proven one. A farmer who is free and owns the land he or she farms has a powerful motivation to take better care of the land and water and to produce more efficiently.

All the evidence tells us that in the long run, freedom from hunger can best be achieved by those governments and citizens who are themselves free. Indeed, there is no more urgent objective for a free society than to break the bonds of hunger. More than half a century ago, Donald Faris, a longtime student of the developing countries, wrote in his book *To Plow with Hope:* "Those of us who have never known real hunger need to remember that to the continuously hungry democracy is senseless unless it brings with it freedom from want." That is why the U.S. Congress has enacted such essential feeding programs as school lunches; food assistance for needy women and infants, and children below the age of five; and food stamps for the poor. Every one of these public programs was enacted by a Congress that was responding to a free electorate. For the same reason, I believe we will soon take steps to end the inexcusable hunger that still afflicts 31 million Americans. No other prosperous, industrialized country permits such an embarrassing problem to exist within its borders.

Naturally, ending hunger in Third World nations will be much more difficult. But freedom from don't-give-a-damn governments can take countries a long way on the road to freedom from hunger. To complete that journey there must be a reduction in—and one hopes an end to—the destructive armed conflicts that have convulsed so much of the Third World. This is proposition number two, which is closely related to proposition one: the achievement of more responsible governments—more democracy. Democracy and peace are the essential handmaidens of freedom from hunger and want.

Unfortunately, in the 1990s, conflicts proliferated, creating more food shortages and hardships in the already hurting Third World. By 1996, violent conflicts had left 80 million additional people facing hunger. Of these, 23 million were war refugees; another 27 million were driven from their homes but remained in their own countries as displaced persons.

"Resolving hostilities and reversing associated agricultural and economic losses are critical if agriculture and human development outlooks are to improve in the 21st Century," the International Food Policy Research Institute (IFPRI) report concludes.

In the last quarter-century, conflicts have driven large numbers of farmers off their land, leaving no one to tend the crops and livestock. This not only impoverishes the refugee farm families, but also obviously diminishes the nation's food supply and its goods for export. Bands of armed men move through the country tearing up property, water systems, and medical clinics; they disrupt the all-important ecological systems. Beyond the slaughter of human beings, these conflicts are destructive almost beyond belief, leaving in their wake blasted villages, roadways sown with land mines, torn-up fields, blackened trees, and polluted waterways.

Another enormous cost of such armed conflicts fought with lethal modern weapons is that the purchase of these weapons eats up money needed for investments in education, health, agriculture, and the protection of the environment. I regret that the United States is the number one arms salesman to the developing world. Instead of selling arms and land mines we ought to lead the way in refusing to worsen hunger in other countries by selling them arms they can't afford for wars they shouldn't fight. We can sell poor countries arms, and they can continue to use them against each other. But that is not the road to freedom from hunger; it is the road to more misery and suffering. Having always believed that I am a citizen of the greatest country on earth, I do not want my great and good land to forget its high ideals in its relations with the developing world. That is what I meant as a presidential nominee in 1972, when I called America home to the ideals that launched the nation in 1776.

One final point concerning conflict: it is probably going to be some years before the developing countries can break free of armed struggle. Therefore, the international community must move to strengthen the World Court and to create an effective international police force under the United Nations. This book is not the place to go into detail on this matter. But neither the United States nor any other country wants to be the world's policeman. This is the responsibility of the United Nations. As Franklin Roosevelt believed, we Americans might well be in the forefront of creating a more effective UN police force. We should also support a stronger World Court instead of weakening the court by ignoring its verdicts, as we have sometimes done in the past. Some Third World disputes could be settled by the court. In the event this does not work and violence erupts, the UN should quickly decide whether to send in an international military force strong enough to end the fighting. Every nation belonging to the UN should make some contribution to the international police force, whether in soldiers or materials or money. This should enable countries to reduce their national armies and arms spending.

In 1974 I served as a U.S. Senate delegate to a world conference on hunger in Rome. There I proposed that every country agree to reduce its arms spending by 10 percent. The savings of many billions of dollars could then be invested in creating an international police force and in a global effort to end hunger. I was pleasantly surprised to learn that simultaneously the delegate from the Vatican released a proposal from His Holiness the Pope almost identical to mine. There had been no discussion between the Vatican and my office; we were simply singing the same hymn that day. I thought we were right then; I still do.

Perhaps it would be appropriate to close this chapter with some words from President Dwight Eisenhower:

> Every gun that is made, every warship launched, every rocket fired signifies, in the final sense, a theft from those who hunger and are not fed, those who are cold and are not clothed.
>
> This world in arms is not spending money alone. It is spending the sweat of its laborers, the genius of its scientists, the hopes of its children. . . . This is not a way of life at all, in any true sense. Under the cloud of threatening war, it is humanity hanging from a cross of iron.

CHAPTER 6

WATER

SHORTLY AFTER I ARRIVED in Rome in the spring of 1998 to take up my post as American ambassador to the FAO, I called on the director general of this oldest and largest of the UN specialized agencies, Dr. Jacques Diouf. Halfway into our conversation I asked my host what he regarded as the most important priorities in winning the battle against hunger. Somewhat to my surprise, but not entirely so, he replied: "The three most important priorities are water, water and water."

Such an assertion can set off intense debates among experts who ascribe hunger to other causes—discrimination against girls and women, armed conflict, bad government, population growth, primitive agriculture, soil erosion, and unjust social and economic orders. But with due regard for these other factors in the world food challenge, it is clear that neither humans nor the farm produce that sustains them can survive without water. It is also a fact that water is not unlimited. Indeed, water is in short supply—critically so—in many parts of the world. The lack of water and the misuse of water may well be the principal cause of hunger.

In 1975, as chairman of the Subcommittee on the Middle East of the Senate Foreign Relations Committee, I went on a mission to the Arab states and Israel. During this trip I was the guest at a small dinner given by the late King Hussein of Jordan and his American wife, Queen Noor. Much of the land I was to visit was desert, parched and dry. During dinner I complimented the King, not only for his efforts toward peace, but also for leading Jordan to a successful economy without the benefit of the vast oil resources enjoyed by some of his fellow Arab states. Always gracious and restrained in conversation, he replied softly: "There are two things more important to this part of the world than oil. The first of these is to secure a just and lasting peace settlement with our neighbors. The second is water. We can live without oil; we cannot live without water and we cannot live without peace."

I thought then and I have thought ever since that this good king was right on the mark that night. It was a short declaration without fanfare from a wise and thoughtful man. I wish he were still alive and advising the international community. His premature death from cancer and the murder of Israeli Prime Minister Itzhak Rabin at the hands of a fanatic deprived the Middle East and the world of two men with a sense of history and destiny. They clearly understood the necessity of both peace and the constructive use and conservation of water in the life of their nations and in the world. Both were weary of hatred and violence. Both longed for the opportunity to lay the foundation for a more secure and prosperous future, free from war and killing. I treasure the conversations I had with these two men on visits to the Middle East and in Washington. They added much to my understanding.

It is perhaps difficult for Americans to think of water shortages. We turn on our taps and our glasses, showers, and bathtubs quickly fill. No problem. We water our lawns and gardens copiously with no thought that the stream from our hoses or sprinklers might stop. The fairways on our beautiful golf courses are as green as always. On our farms and ranches the cattle tanks are full. U.S. irrigation water and that of the rest of the world combined is the largest human use of water on our planet—it flows over vast stretches of productive croplands, gardens, vineyards, and orchards, some in deserts. Our schools, hospitals, prisons, shops, and factories are never without water. Needless to say, no one expects the fire department to run out of water. As for America's beautiful rivers, parks, public pools, and recreational sites—surely they won't run dry. Of course, many Americans have experienced temporary water shortages. We have been asked to cut back on watering our lawns. And residents of California and other parts of the West know firsthand the growing concern over water. But I suspect that most Americans worry very little about the availability of water.

So why are the director general of the UN Food and Agriculture Organization and the late King Hussein and some of our most respected scientists and farsighted statesmen warning us that water is the supreme crisis of the near future?

Consider the words of Paul Simon of Illinois, one of the most thoughtful and levelheaded men ever to serve in the U.S. Senate:

> "By the gift of water you nourish and sustain us and all living things." These are the words used in the baptismal rite in Lutheran services. But in our world, increasing numbers of people cannot assume they will be nourished and sustained. Within a few years, a water crisis of catastrophic proportions will

explode on us—unless aroused citizens in this and other nations demand of their leadership actions reflecting vision, understanding and courage.

It is no exaggeration to say that the conflict between humanity's growing thirst and the projected supply of usable, potable water could result in the most devastating natural disaster since history has been recorded accurately, unless something happens to stop it (*Parade* magazine, Aug. 23, 1998).

These are strong words to come from a reflective man not known for his purple prose. So are the observations by the editors of the *New York Times* published on the eve of a March 2000 conference in Amsterdam attended by water ministers from more than 100 nations. As the *Times* noted: half the world's 6 billion people have no sanitary way to dispose of their bodily waste; 1.3 billion have no safe source of drinking water.

I have seen children and adults drinking from stagnant pools and other sources that were visibly polluted. Humans who are sufficiently thirsty will consume water from sickening sources. More than 4 million people die each year of waterborne diseases. Indeed, unsanitary water is the source of 90 percent of all cases of infectious diseases in the developing world. AIDS is a terrifying killer, especially in Africa, but it kills far fewer people than dirty water. The annual kill rate is now 2.9 million for AIDS and 4 million–plus for bad water.

UN authorities estimate that it will cost an additional $9 billion annually to provide safe, clean water and adequate sanitation facilities for everyone. As the *Times* editors conclude in their impressive summary of the world's water challenge: "No other investment would buy more health for less money." Nine billion dollars is, of course, a lot of money for the United Nations to raise above its present budget. The American share, roughly 25 percent, would be about $2.2 billion—again, a lot of money: about the cost of a B-2 bomber.

Before we further probe this quietly developing crisis, let me make clear that it can be avoided or at least made manageable if we have leadership that comprehends the challenge and possesses the courage to act decisively in the next decade or two. But we must first understand some of the dimensions of the problem.

We begin with the knowledge that the present global population of 6 billion is expected to reach 8 billion by 2030 and 10 billion by the year 2050 when it is expected to level off. Those figures may drop, as previously noted, if the educational level of the Third World rises, especially among girls. It is of course true that as the global population increases, water consumption will also have to increase. But it is a matter of concern that as matters now stand per capita water consumption is increasing at a rate double that of the population growth rate.

This rapid increase in water consumption per person would not be so dangerous if the world's supply of usable water were infinite. Astronauts looking down on our planet with its huge oceans might get the impression that our planet is a ball of water. But less than 1 percent of that water is now available for human needs. Like tillable soil, usable water is a limited resource. It is much too valuable to waste or pollute.

Not surprisingly, agriculture is by far the biggest user of water. Two-thirds of the water taken from our planet's lakes, rivers, and underground aquifers is used to irrigate crops. An estimated one-third of global food production comes from irrigated acres. More than two-thirds of the needed additional food production in the Third World will necessarily come from irrigated fields.

Already, twenty developing countries face critical water shortages. In these countries there is not enough water to produce crops sufficient to feed the people. In many countries, water has been improperly used, the result being the erosion or destruction of much of the soil. This threatens the sustainability of food production.

Nearly two-thirds of the water used for irrigation is lost in runoffs, seeping back into the soil and causing waterlogging and salinity. Twenty-five years ago in Iraq, I saw devastating damage to the soil caused by improper management of irrigation flows from the Euphrates and Tigris Rivers. It is estimated that a fourth of all the irrigated land in the Third World is damaged, its productivity diminished or destroyed, because of stagnant, wasted water and salinization.

But again, Jacques Diouf writes in an important FAO report, *Crops and Drops,* that his agency "is confident that the global food supply can keep pace with population growth in the years to come if the political will exists to implement the necessary measures. 'More crop per drop' will require efficient and productive use of agricultural water." Some of the world's best engineers, as well as soil and water experts, must guide the work on this large part of the water and food challenge. Fortunately, some of them are already engaged in this task.

Looking ahead, perhaps fifteen years or so, one could say that whereas in the past nations have gone to war over oil, the greater danger ahead will be war over water. U.S. intelligence experts have identified a dozen or more flashpoints where, a few years down the road, war could break out over water control.

Water

In the previous chapter I wrote of the crying need to reduce the conflict, killing, and destruction in the Third
World if the world's people are to break free from hunger.
This concern is related to the water crisis because some of
the most troublesome frictions and conflict points center
on the competition for water. One such danger point in-
volves India, Pakistan, and Bangladesh. These three countries, which historically have suffered from disputes over a
number of issues, are all heavily dependent on agriculture
for their survival. All three draw vital water from the same
rivers and underground sources, and these are pressed to
their limits. Historical tensions between these states have
been aggravated recently by nuclear weapons.

If there is a flashpoint that could trigger a military out-
burst, possibly escalating to nuclear exchanges, it might well
be control of water in this teeming region of South Asia.
What a cruel irony if millions—perhaps tens of millions—
of men, women, and children should lose their lives in a nuclear war fought to control life-giving water. It would be
even more ironic if the water of the region were poisoned
by nuclear fallout, as almost certainly would be the case.
Nuclear explosions poison, incinerate, melt, or pulverize
everything on the scene and for long distances in every direction.

In the Middle East, King Hussein said shortly before his
death that water is the issue that "could drive the nations of
this region to war." Former Israeli prime minister Benjamin
Netanyahu said that "Israel is headed toward a mess in water." Quite clearly, the Israelis, the Jordanians, the Palestini-
ans, and the Syrians all have a jealous eye on the water of
the Jordan River. Further north, Turkey largely controls the
life-giving flow of the Euphrates River to Iraq and other
states. What happens if growing water needs in Turkey

prompt that nation's government to slow or halt the flow of the Euphrates to other countries that depend on this vital source?

Egypt has tried hard in recent years to achieve peace in the Middle East. But this ancient nation has its own problems—including water. It is difficult to think of a region whose well-being is more dependent upon a river than Egypt with its beloved Nile. In a sense, the Nile *is* Egypt. But 85 percent of the water of this life-sustaining river comes from Ethiopia. What happens when the population of Ethiopia doubles, as now seems certain, and begins to use more and more of the water that now sustains Egypt's growing population and its agriculture along the Nile?

Three hundred of China's cities and the country's one billion people face serious water shortages. How will the tough dictatorship of this huge country respond?

More than 200 of the world's rivers supply water to two or more countries. Each one of these life-sustaining streams is a potential battlefield if a more intense competition for water is allowed to develop between hard-pressed governments backed by their desperate citizenry. If men are willing to fight for boundaries and flags, land and oil, they will certainly be ready to fight for water. War is not pleasant, but neither is thirsting to death, or watching one's children die of thirst, or of starvation brought on by the lack of water needed to produce food.

What can be done to replace the danger of new wars with a constructive and satisfactory solution to the impending water shortage?

We Americans are tremendously blessed by the richness of our resources, including water. No other country has such an abundance of rich soil, pure water, forests, minerals, mountains, grasslands, wildlife, and fisheries. But we still have to exercise greater care in the use and conservation of these resources—especially water.

Three of our fastest-growing states—Florida, Texas, and California—are now feeling the pinch of water scarcity. Arizona, New Mexico, Nevada, and Utah also face the beginnings of water shortages. These problems will worsen as the demand for water increases with the growth in population, industry, and irrigation. Perhaps our most populous state, California, has the severest looming water crisis.

But solving water problems in the United States is comparatively easy. Conservation within reason must become the order of the day in the big water-problem states—California, Texas and Florida. These states are all logical candidates for the desalination of the vast ocean tides that lap along their shores. Desalination is not cheap, but neither are the warships, jet bombers, submarines, missiles, and tanks that continuously roll off our defense plant lines. Does anyone believe that this costly military equipment is any more essential to our security and survival than water? Yes, desalination costs money, but it is a proven success as a source of drinkable and usable water. We live in the world's richest nation, with huge oceans east and west. We can tighten our belts a little and pay whatever is necessary to assure ourselves an adequate water supply.

The problem is obviously tougher in most of the rest of the world—the Middle East, Asia, Africa, and Latin America. The water problem is more serious in these areas partly because most of the people are poor. They don't have the means to secure dependable water. It is estimated by FAO sources that a billion people do not have access to clean, safe water. Usually the poorest of the poor are the women and children. They are less likely than the men to have money and mobility, and so they suffer most. Of course, if a water problem persists, everyone eventually suffers.

The most experienced and knowledgeable people with whom I have conferred at the UN agencies in Rome all tell me that, difficult though it may be, the Third World water problem can be solved. That prediction depends on several steps:

(1) There must be a strong effort to conserve water in every possible way, but especially the huge volume of agricultural irrigation water. The FAO has the technical people and the know-how to assist this effort. Once irrigation reaches the fields and provides water for the crops, the runoff should be captured and reused rather than collecting in stagnant pools that ruin the soil. Farmers can be taught how to achieve such economical use of water both by UN agencies and through individual national efforts such as the U.S. Farmers Corps I proposed in point 4 of the first chapter. Many farmers in the United States and other developed countries have learned how to manage water wisely. If a number of these older, experienced farmers were to sign up for service in an international Farmers Corps, they could offer invaluable help to Third World farmers in the conservation and prudent use of water resources.

(2) Wherever feasible, the developing countries, with the assistance of the advanced countries and the UN, should be encouraged to develop desalination plants. The considerable capital required could come from the World Bank, which under its brilliant president, James Wolfensen, is making such constructive investments. The International Monetary Fund can also help with needed capital, as can affluent countries such as Japan, Germany, France, England, Italy, Canada, Australia, Taiwan, South Korea, and the United

States, and perhaps such oil-rich countries as Kuwait and Saudi Arabia. Places as diverse as Israel and St. Croix, one of the American Virgin Islands, are already successfully using desalination.

(3) Family planning on a wider scale, with the resultant lowering of the birthrate, can contribute in important ways to relieving the pressure on water resources and the food supply. Beyond these considerations, those who have a reverence for the lives of women and children should not wish to see them jeopardized by excessive birthrates that exhaust young mothers, diminish their ability to care for their children, and place further demands on limited food and water.

The FAO has recently completed a study of ninety-three selected developing countries which concluded that over the next thirty years the effective irrigated area of the Third World can be increased 34 percent with the use of only 12 percent more water. How can this be? Two factors are influential here.

First, changing food habits of people in the developing countries are reducing the amount of water needed for producing food crops. For example, rice is a crop that requires large amounts of water, about twice as much per acre as wheat. As people are converted from eating rice to eating wheat products, as is now happening in the developing countries, less irrigation water is needed.

Second, and more important, the FAO scientists and technicians have concluded that the efficiency with which irrigation water is used can be greatly increased over the coming thirty years.

I am not a scientist, an agriculturist, or a water engineer, but I have visited enough developing countries over the years in the company of men and women who are experts in these fields to be persuaded by the optimism of the FAO analysis. With sufficient effort and brain power, we can win the effort to achieve water security within thirty years.

IT IS IMPORTANT to remember that while irrigation is crucial to farming in the developing world, as it is in more developed countries, rainfall direct from the skies is still, everywhere, the largest and most important source of water for crops. This pure life-giving water must be offered at least as much attention in its efficient use and conservation as is given to irrigation water from rivers, lakes, and underground aquifers.

If the most efficient use of water is to help ending world hunger, certain facts must be kept in mind. Of all the world's cropland, 17 percent is irrigated; this 17 percent provides approximately 40 percent of world food production. The remaining 60 percent of the world's food comes from rain-fed agriculture. In water-scarce tropical regions such as sub-Saharan Africa, nearly all of the cropland (more than 95 percent) is rain-fed and will remain so as the dominant source of food for growing populations.

Let us consider some of the misuses of fresh rainwater and irrigation water, and then examine some of the improvements that can be made. Too much water at the wrong time and too little water at the wrong time have been the curse of agriculture. I do not forget the scenes of my childhood—farmers nervously deploring the excess of rain that soaked their fields and kept them from getting in their crops at planting time, and later the same farmers anxiously scanning cloudless skies for rain that did not come in time to save their crops. To varying degrees it's the same all over the world. Hardworking farmers are anxious everywhere.

Sometimes wasteful use in one area deprives other areas of desperately needed water. Misuse also occurs when clean water is utilized and then returned to the water system in a polluted condition. Used irrigation water is frequently contaminated by salts, pesticides, and herbicides, which make it useless to other farmers. Likewise, the fast-growing urban and industrial centers around the world in too many instances dump contaminated water both into surface bodies and into underground aquifers.

Some of the most glaring examples of the misuse of both rainwater and irrigation water are found in such river basins as the Huang Hai, the Colorado, the Shabeelle, and the great Yellow River in China, all of which dry up before they reach the sea because of correctable overuse and misuse.

In 1997 the Yellow River was dried up and did not complete its descent to the sea for seven months. Consider what this grim situation meant to the millions of farmers and workers who live along the lower reaches of the river. As the FAO experts note: "Dried up rivers are a good example of the overuse of freshwater supplies. Overuse in one place means deprivation in others. The flat fertile deltas of many rivers were once centers of high agricultural production. Where the rivers no longer flow, water for irrigation becomes unavailable, farmers go out of business and local production fails."

The basic cause of this condition is usually upstream development that does not properly consider downstream results. There is an urgent need for more attention to the basin-wide requirements of river systems. As matters now stand, careless upstream agricultural practices, plus logging and unplanned road building, are all producing dangerous soil erosion. This, in turn, clogs rivers and reservoirs with sediment that causes flooding in midstream and reduces water flows downstream.

Irrigation water, if not properly managed, can undermine food production and damage the environment. When upstream farmers overuse irrigation, they can produce a crop in a comparatively small area, only to choke off water to much larger marginal areas needed for food production. Beyond this, irrigation water drawn too carelessly from rivers and lakes threatens the aquatic ecosystems needed for wetlands and thus produces losses in biodiversity, the purification of water systems, and, in the long run, food productivity.

Before leaving the water crisis, it may be useful to look at one of our planet's most devastating agricultural and environmental disasters: the Aral Sea, located in Kazak on the southern rim of Russia. Until about forty years ago, the Aral Sea was fed year-round by the Amu Darya River. In recent decades nearly the river's entire flow has been diverted to irrigate cotton plantations (rather than for production of food). As a consequence, a large, beautiful, and productive lake has dried up. Twenty of the twenty-four species of edible fish have vanished. The catch, which totaled 44,000 tons annually in the 1950s and produced 60,000 jobs, has dropped to nothing—no fish, no jobs. Deadly salt-dust mixtures blown out of the dead seabed fall across surrounding areas, damaging or killing essential food crops. The sluggish river carries salts and toxic chemicals, making the water dangerous to drink and spreading diseases along its path. Those who have remained in the area are impoverished and hungry, having lost their major source of food and water. Those who have deserted the once productive river and lake system have become environmental refugees. A similar fate awaits farmers on the deltas of many rivers from which so much water has been heedlessly drawn upstream as to leave little for potentially more productive land downstream. Clearly, this results in a reduction of overall food output.

These are not simply the technical terms of bureaucrats; they represent serious life-and-death threats to millions of people. Multitudes of men, women, and children who once depended on inland fisheries as a key source of protein have watched as much of this important food supply has been destroyed by improper water management. The natural filtering action of wetlands, which for countless generations has cleaned up much of the world's wastewater, has been weakened or destroyed in all too many areas. Again, this is not the contention of so-called environmental elitists; it is hard scientific fact with a deeply human impact.

In every case that I know of where wetlands have been destroyed for irrigation or for other reasons, the results have been deeply regretted. The Salish and Flathead Indian tribes of Montana suffered heavily when a poorly conceived federal dam led to the loss of their wetlands—their source of fish and wildlife. The Indians took their case to court and the court ruled that they were entitled to $35 million in damages.

Chemicals used in farming frequently pollute irrigation runoff, which, in turn, can contaminate precious groundwater. Fertilizer containing potassium and nitrogen, whether on rain-fed or irrigated land, often finds its way into surface water or groundwater, producing long-term environmental and agricultural destruction. Such contaminated water sometimes produces algae blooms and eutrophication, a process that depletes shallow waters of oxygen during the summer.

The FAO report *Crops and Drops* concludes: "Overuse

of limited water supplies is exacerbated by waste, which occurs at almost every point at which humans interfere with
the natural water cycle. Irrigation is notoriously wasteful:
water is wasted at almost every point in the cycle, from the
leaking canals that are used to supply irrigation water to the
huge volumes of water that fall uselessly on soil where there
are no crops or which are in excess of the amount required
by the crop. Improving irrigation efficiency is a key goal for
the future."

Recently, I came across a study by my FAO associates
which analyzes a final cause of the water and food crisis: the
dramatic increase in so-called natural disasters. Many of
these disasters are not "natural" at all, but the result of careless human stewardship of the land, forests, and water. But
the FAO report is correct when it asserts: "It will prove impossible to maximize agricultural production from limited
water supplies unless the factors that so accentuate the ef-
fects of natural disasters can be corrected." In other words,
these disasters are not entirely the result of Mother Nature
or the Almighty. They won't be cured by prayer or consul-
tations with the Fairy Godmother.

A recent study by the Munich Re Group, a well-
regarded research institute, reveals that the number of natural
disasters such as floods, mud slides, storms, and earthquakes
has increased more than threefold from the 1960s to the
1990s. The economic damage caused by these catastrophes
in that same period has increased nearly ninefold.

But floods, and the mud slides that frequently accom-
pany them, even in such exalted precincts as Malibu Beach
and Beverly Hills, likely result from man's folly rather than
God's wrath. It is not too much to contend that these disasters can largely be prevented by using our God-given brains

and common sense. God doesn't want to cover us with mud; He wants us to live cleanly and abundantly to glorify Him and all his wonderful works. The prophet Isaiah promises us that God's creatures should neither "hunger nor thirst . . . for he that hath mercy on them shall lead them, even by the springs of water shall he guide them" (Isaiah 49:10).

Floods and mud slides occur, and will do so increasingly, because of the degradation of land by improper agricultural and industrial practices, practices that can be corrected by the same people who engage in them. Approximately three-fourths of drylands in the world and one-sixth of the planet's population are being seriously damaged by land degradation and floods that we humans know how to prevent if we have the political will to do so. Most of this damage is confined to drought-prone areas in Africa, South Asia, and South America. In the past thirty years millions of people have needlessly lost their livelihoods and their lives because of the degradation of once-productive land.

Consider this terse conclusion by the UN Food and Agriculture Organization, published on the occasion of World Food Day in 1994: "In many parts of the world, rain-fed cropland is in poor shape. Increasing human and live-stock populations have led to land degradation through soil erosion, overgrazing, bush fires, deforestation and the expansion of arable farming onto unsuitable marginal land. In arid and semi-arid areas, which cover a third of the Earth's land surface, these forms of degradation lead to deserts."

The cost in suffering is nearly unbearable. The African droughts of 1984–85 seriously weakened or killed 35 million people; land degradation, a major cause of floods and mud slides all over the world, as well as of recurring drought and the creation of sterile deserts, caused some 10 million people to flee their homelands and become environmental refugees.

In 1998 human mistakes greatly aggravated the death and destruction caused by El Niño and its related Hurricane Mitch. Mud slides raced down slopes that had been denuded by ill-advised deforestation and the attempted farming of highly marginal land. Flooding was worsened by the lack of watershed planning and management.

So what can be done? Earlier in this chapter, I briefly mentioned three helpful steps: (1) a greater effort to conserve water everywhere, from New York to New Delhi; (2) the development of desalination plants for countries that border the oceans; and (3) the extension of family planning worldwide as a humane and commonsense course if the pressure on food and water supplies is to be relieved. But with or without family planning, which will come inevitably, albeit slowly, no matter what course religious spokesmen take, there are important steps to be taken on the water and food front.

For many years farmers in more advanced countries, such as the United States, have been able to increase production with less damage to soil and water because they have seized on the findings of science. The same findings should and must be more widely shared and applied in the Third World if we are to curb the present wasteful and discouraging misuse of land and water. There is only so much backbreaking labor that men and women can bring to land and water. Then they must call on the scientists, the agronomists, the water engineers, and experienced farmers elsewhere who can bring the wisdom and knowledge that come from a lifetime of working with soil, seeds, weather, and water.

Water

As a science novice, not always able to grasp its intricacies, I nonetheless believe that science will one day find the answer to AIDS just as it has found solutions or partial solutions to malaria, tuberculosis, polio, diphtheria, diabetes, muscular dystrophy, heart disease, and cancer. I have prayed, especially since 1994 when a precious daughter died of alcoholism, that we may some day find an answer even to that terrible affliction.

I'm sure that scientists working with experienced farmers can one day soon point the way to safer and healthier irrigation; wiser management of river basins, lakes, oceans, and rainfall; and more effective protection and management of the land, the forests, and our global environment.

I have mentioned the many problems that afflict the earth's water and land, on which our capacity to feed ourselves depends. I believe strongly that each of these problems can be greatly ameliorated in the next thirty years. We have the capacity to accomplish that. Every informed person I have worked with in Rome, in Washington, and in South Dakota tells me that there is enough food in the world and enough productive potential to end humanity's hunger. Do we have the political and moral will? This is the question that I cannot answer with certainty. The answer depends on what kind of leadership arises both in the developing countries and in the advantaged nations. We know that some Third World governments seem indifferent to hunger and poverty. But even in these countries, citizens can form cooperative local associations to make better use of their water, land, fisheries, and forests.

Here are some of the constructive steps that might be carried out peacefully despite corrupt or indifferent central governments. Consider improvements in irrigation that farmers, aided by a local citizens' group, might sponsor: (1) reducing seepage and other wasteful losses of water in irrigation channels by lining those channels or using pipelines; (2) reducing the loss of water from evaporation by avoiding irrigation during the most intense sunlight hours and by using undercanopy devices that direct the water into the soil rather than into the air as do overhead sprinklers; (3) avoiding excessive irrigation; (4) controlling weeds on interrow strips and keeping strips dry; (5) planting and harvesting at optimal times, to reduce water waste and the chance of crop failure; (6) irrigating frequently, with no more water than is necessary to keep the crop growing.

In Turkey, the government has wisely turned over to local farmers' associations almost the entire management of irrigation systems. The same transfer has happened in Mexico, with 85 percent of the publicly irrigated land now being successfully managed by associations that include both men and women. Experienced farmers on the scene have a better grasp of how water can be most effectively used than do governments far from the local farmers and often indifferent to their needs.

Still another wise step that can be executed by individual farmers with the cooperation of local citizens' associations is the construction of tanks and reservoirs to store irrigation runoff and wet-season rainfall so that the water can be used in dry seasons. This may seem like obvious common sense—it must surely be done throughout the Third World. Not so. There is an urgent need to devise more systems to store rainwater and irrigation runoff to provide water for livestock and for farm homes, as well as to offset the dry spells that can otherwise destroy crops.

Also, with the rapid growth of urban centers in the developing countries, there are new sources of wastewater that can be directed to irrigated cropland around the cities. Most of the wastewater in cities ends up in the public sewerage system. If this water were properly treated and used again, not for drinking, cooking, or washing, but in controlled irrigation, it could effectively sustain hundreds of farms. The fertilizer value of the effluent might be nearly as great as the value of the water itself. Such cooperation between city and country can be rewarding everywhere. It reminds farmers and urbanites that they can be partners rather than mutual suspects or even enemies. There has always, everywhere, been a certain tension and friction between town and country. Here is one way of easing those tensions for the greater good of all.

Democratic associations of farmers and urbanites are also needed to establish priority uses for the resources of the river basins. I am not thinking of such gigantic creations as the marvelous Tennessee Valley Authority—a regional entity with strong local input that has coordinated a great river's irrigation, flood control, hydroelectric power, and recreational features. These multiple uses of the great Tennessee River have transformed a once impoverished section of the nation into a prosperous agricultural and industrial giant. Many visitors who have come from all over the world to view and study the Tennessee Valley Authority have come away believing they have seen one of the great man-made wonders of our age. They are probably right in that assessment. But most of the Third World is not ready to build and absorb such a huge development. Nor are the billions of dollars available to finance such a project.

But there are other developments ordinary people can set in motion at the local and regional levels to utilize better the resources of their river basins. As matters now stand, there is no logical water-use plan for most of these waterways in the developing countries. Water is simply drawn from the river basin willy-nilly without regard to priorities. In many cases central governments are far removed and indifferent to such local matters. But local people—women and men—cannot afford to be indifferent. They need to associate together, elect officers, and set up priorities and purposes for the potentially rich water systems in which they live. Final decisions should be approved by the votes of all the men and women who make up the association. This is grassroots democracy—like American rural electric cooperatives, like the urban merchant associations that enable businesspeople to work together to improve business opportunities and jobs in their communities.

One possible plan of action for a river basin association might be as follows: the purest water should be used for drinking, cooking, and bathing in cities and on farms; domestic wastewater could then be directed to the irrigation of crops, such as cereals; finally, the poorest-quality water could be used to irrigate forests, plantations, pastureland, parks, gardens, and lawns.

I do not want to make all of this sound too simple. Many waterways are shared by two or more countries. Forty-seven percent of the world's land is in international river basins, of which there are more than 200. Thirteen of these rivers embrace five or more countries. In these instances, local associations will not be enough without the cooperation of central governments. But local associations can raise localized hell (without violence) until their governments awaken to see what is going on down the river.

The big three in river basin usage are urban, industrial, and agricultural users. They will all get bigger and more demanding. But there are still other users who must be heeded: electric utilities, which may require hydroelectric power like that created by the Missouri River in South Dakota and the neighboring states. Water may also be needed to cool either conventional or nuclear power plants; port authorities will be asking for water to sustain navigation; wetlands will have to be assigned water to do their marvelous work of filtering out impurities and sustaining wildlife; and downstream fisherfolk are entitled to a river flow that sustains this essential source of low-cholesterol, low-fat, high-protein food, the humble fish.

Another reason for democratic action at the local level is to establish organized incentives for users of resources to practice conservation and avoid waste. To begin with, most government subsidies to irrigation users should be stopped. There may be justification for continuing some of these subsidies, but for the most part they only encourage the waste of irrigation water by selling it too cheaply. Pricing of irrigation water to farmers should be set by a local committee of men and women that rewards farmers with lower water prices for careful, economical use and penalizes them with higher prices if they waste water. The farmer who uses the most water per acre compared with his neighbors should be charged a higher fee. These practices can be observed and reported by the locally constituted association, with the user given the right of appeal. If the farmer in question reduces his volume of water use per acre and still secures a good crop, he should then be rewarded with a lower water charge. People in the field who have seen this price incentive system in operation tell me that it greatly reduces the waste of both water and land.

"Study how a society uses its land, and you can come to pretty reliable conclusions as to what its future will be," observed E. F. Schumacher in his classic little book, *Small Is Beautiful*. Schumacher would be quick to add that water and land management are inseparable twins walking hand in hand into the future, for good or ill, depending on how wisely governments and citizens use these life-sustaining resources. Are we equal to that summons to responsibility and common sense?

CHAPTER 7

ENDING WORLD HUNGER
IN OUR TIME

"Now this is not the end. It is not even the beginning of the end. But it is perhaps the end of the beginning." So said Winston Churchill in a 1943 wartime radio
address to his people.

Now, at the age of seventy-eight, I do not expect to see
the end of world hunger—unless the good Lord extends
my years beyond 100. But I do intend to complain loudly
to St. Peter if I am called above (or raise the devil, if I'm
called below) before we end hunger in America. I also expect to see us reach well past "the end of the beginning" of
our victory over *world* hunger. If we can now reach other
planets thanks to the scientific genius of our space archi-
tects, there is no acceptable reason why this planet should
still have millions of hungry and starving men, women, and
children by the year 2030. That gives us three decades—
which will pass all too quickly—to achieve what will surely
be the greatest victory in world history. Wherever I am in
the world beyond, if such there be, when my fellow humans
are finally emancipated from hunger, I'm going to lead a
chorus of celebration: Hallelujah! Hallelujah!

To reach that day, we will require not only the help of scientists but also the grassroots participation of men and women in local water and land user associations, in the management of local irrigation districts, and in decisions as to how the resources of the great river basins are used. It was a group of scientists who staged the Green Revolution, but the food and agriculture revolution of the next three decades will triumph only if land and water management becomes everyone's business.

"Everyone's business" includes women equally with men. "Everyone" embraces the poor as well as the rich. The scientists and other experts who drafted the invaluable report previously cited, *Crops and Drops,* conclude: "There is no room in an efficient water [and land] management scheme for elitist roles for the wealthy or socially distinguished; often, the people who most need a new say in how water [and land] [are] managed, and who know most how [they] should be managed, are poor women smallholders." To that I offer a ringing amen. Gender and class equality in decision-making is essential to the victory over hunger.

A keener sense of social and economic justice across the whole spectrum of society in the developing countries is crucial to ending poverty and hunger. That sense of justice must empower poor people to shape their own destiny. Self-determination is the watchword of freedom and the path to a more just and equitable society. It is also the way to freedom from hunger.

It is significant that a whole series of careful FAO studies has shown that small landholders produce more food per acre than do larger landholders. Data coming recently from India, Pakistan, Bangladesh, Sri Lanka, and the Philippines demonstrates that small landholders are more careful than large ones in water usage, manage their irrigated croplands more efficiently, apply fertilizer with greater care, and grow more diversified, higher-value crops with more reliance on their own labor rather than machinery. A recent FAO study found that small landowners produced more per acre in thirty-nine of fifty-five developing countries. In the other sixteen countries, the results were less conclusive, but the overall findings were a clear win for the efficiency of small family-type farming.

Long ago I concluded that the best and most efficient farmers in South Dakota and the nation lived and worked on family farms—meaning farms small enough to be cultivated by a single family while providing the family with most of its income. This tradition, which has made American farmers the envy of the world, was enshrined in the landmark Homestead Act in 1862 during the administration of President Abraham Lincoln. This act offered any settler 160 acres of public land if he or she was willing to live on the acreage and cultivate it. In that same year, two other agricultural landmarks—perhaps overshadowed by the Civil War—were achieved: the creation of the state land-grant colleges with their agricultural experiment stations, and the launching of the U.S. Department of Agriculture with full Cabinet status. The experience of all three of these great building blocks in the success of American agriculture should be offered to (not pushed or forced on) the developing countries.

I urge the full involvement of farmers and their spouses in the management of land and water resources partly because I have watched such essentially political grassroots practices work so well in my state and across the land. Consider, for example, the Rural Electric Cooperatives launched in the 1930s. They enabled American farm families to band together in cooperative associations, elect their own leaders and managers, borrow federal funds at low interest rates, and then bring electrical power to the previously dark farms and homes of rural America. Almost without exception, those farmer-owned and farmer-operated cooperatives have been models of self-help and sound management, including nearly 100 percent repayment of the government loans and interest.

I have been flying airplanes since my nineteenth birthday. In early night flights over my home state and neighboring states, I saw a landscape that was black in all directions except for the towns and cities. From the air, the feeble light cast by kerosene lanterns in farmhouses and barns was not visible. And then came the Rural Electric Cooperatives. Soon South Dakota was lit from border to border with electric bulbs in the homes and barns and farmyards. A pilot crossing the state at night now looked down on a sea of lights that illuminated the landscape. What could not be seen from the air were the electrically powered washing machines and dryers, the feed grinders and milking machines, the radio and television sets, the electric irons and refrigerators, the toasters and hair curlers—and everything else that heretofore was confined to the cities.

The farm families who developed and managed these wonderful electric cooperatives not only enriched their lives with low-cost electric power; they also empowered themselves politically and economically by democratically taking charge of an important part of their lives. It is this kind of empowerment of the even poorer and more deprived people of the developing countries that must take place if they are to climb Jacob's ladder to salvation from hunger.

If American farmers can band together to light their farms—a task which large private utilities spurned because they believed it unprofitable—then similar farmer-run programs can work in managing water, land, irrigation, storage, reservoirs, and profitable public food markets in developing countries. The more democracy and equality of participation, the greater the chances for success.

In the dark days of the 1930s depression, Emil Loriks, a great leader of the South Dakota Farmers Union, told his fellow farmers: "We must build economic power through economic organization—through cooperation." That was also the message of Jim Patton, the colorful president of the National Farmers Union, and M. W. Thatcher, who brilliantly headed the Farmers Union Grain Terminal Association in St. Paul. All three of these men along with the courageous editor of my hometown paper, W. R. Ronald, were my friends and inspirations as long as they lived. I also have a continuing debt for any insights I may have to Dwayne Andreas, the heart and soul of one of our great food and agricultural companies—Archer Daniels Midland. Few if any Americans have a wiser view of the themes treated in this book than does Dwayne Andreas. The message of these great men now needs to be heeded across the developing world.

The Third World has more than its share of corrupt governments and ruling cliques that seek to exploit the people and resources of their countries. These governments are not interested in accountability or in open, transparent behavior. Thieving rulers who ride around in limousines to visit their posh estates at the public's expense don't want either auditors or an alert citizenry examining their behavior.

That is another reason why in some countries it is especially important for people to develop their own grassroots management associations at the local level. Control at the community level of water and land, fisheries and forests is a key factor in all of this. It can be accomplished, but it will be a strenuous test of courage and political will. Victory in these matters must finally come if we are to end hunger in our time.

In the previous chapter I related how citizens can help to control their lives by forming cooperative water management organizations at the community level. Unfortunately, we can't count on all of the Third World governments to lead the way on these vital issues. Too many governments are the enemies of the public interest and the effort to free the world from hunger. It will be better, however, if the people living under such regimes try to bring about needed political change without resorting to violence. Usually violence breeds more violence, and it is the most vulnerable people who will suffer the most, especially the children, the women, and the elderly.

Perhaps the most promising activities for men and women organized in local associations are the child-feeding proposals made earlier in this volume. I strongly believe that the nourishment of both school-age and preschool children, along with pregnant and nursing mothers, is the wisest investment that can be made in the developing world. It is the best way to encourage and underwrite education, which, in turn, leads to smaller, better conducted families and more successful community development.

The most practical way to undertake such a commitment is to begin with the schools, supplemented by local parent-teacher associations. Schools offer a structure and an organization already in place to which school-age children can be attracted and where they can be fed. I know of no school feeding program—providing either breakfast or lunch—that did not result in a substantial increase in school attendance and better academic performance, with less tardiness and fewer dropouts.

I recommend that every aspect of the school lunch program pass muster with a local parent-teacher association— and if there is a school board, with it, too. These folks on the scene, in the homes and in the schools, will know better what kind of school feeding plan best meets the needs of their children and the community.

The United Nations World Food Program, with its experienced network of field workers in eighty countries, is the obvious agency to administer and supervise a global child-feeding program. No other institution has the trained personnel and the accepted multinational strength for this gigantic task. But other organizations can help. As I noted earlier, many private voluntary organizations, such as Catholic Relief Services, Church World Service, Lutheran World Relief, the Mennonite Central Kitchen, the Joint Distribution Committee, the American Friends Service Committee, and CARE have operated for years all over the world. They know how to set up and, if necessary, run school lunch or breakfast programs, and do it well with no graft. This helps their members ensure a place in heaven. But it also ensures that the right food will be served in the right way with low overhead.

Preschool feeding programs and supplementary feeding and nutritional guidance for young mothers do not offer the in-place structures that schools can provide for their child-feeding programs. But, as previously suggested, if local associations were so inclined, it might be possible for young mothers, their infants, and preschool children to come to the school at a given time for supplementary feeding and nutritional counseling. Additional food, for the weekends and other meals, could be sent home with the mothers. Local associations might well devise alternative plans better suited to local conditions for these all-important preschool feedings.

143

AN INCREASINGLY important factor in resolving the world's food challenge will be the role of international trade and investment. It is important for the World Trade Organization's members and leadership to have a comprehensive appreciation of the agricultural, food, and trading requirements of the developing countries. Global trading alone cannot end hunger and poverty even in such an advanced, highly competitive nation as the United States, to say nothing of the impoverished countries of the Third World. But an international trading system that is responsive to the special needs of developing countries can help significantly in the battle against hunger. It has taken many years for the advanced industrial states to understand and profitably work through the international market—a fiercely competitive, complicated jungle to the inexperienced seller or buyer. The developing countries will need the counsel of trading experts from the international organizations, including the World Trade Organization, the World Bank, the International Monetary Fund, the UN Development Program, and the UN Food and Agriculture Organization, plus the assistance of the developed countries.

The 1996 World Food Summit held in Rome recognized the trading vulnerability of the least advanced states. There is an urgent need for specialists to explain to potential Third World traders the advantages of belonging to the World Trade Organization. Developing countries need to have their interested people assisted by outside specialists so that future trade won't leave them at a disadvantage. Regulations, techniques, and hazards involved in multilateral world trade are a test even for the experts of the advanced nations. Imagine the uncertainty, confusion, and outright fear of a half-educated, inexperienced person in Africa, Asia, or Latin America trying to sort out the pitfalls and opportunities of the global trading system. In the United States, we have people who understand these issues thoroughly. One such man is former U.S. Secretary of the Treasury Robert Rubin. I wish he were still in government. But perhaps he and others would be willing to give some of their time and counsel to developing countries.

There is, of course, a strong temptation for advanced countries with extensive experience in trading and monetary affairs to exploit less knowledgeable and more vulnerable people in the less-developed countries. But these temptations must be resisted if developing nations are to succeed in the emerging global economy.

The protests in Seattle in November 1999 saw many thousands of people demonstrating their disapproval of the World Trade Organization and expressing some of the above concerns. They manifested strong objections to business conglomerates arbitrarily moving their industrial plants into Third World countries, there to recruit cheap labor and then undersell companies in countries where workers are paid a more respectable wage. Similar concerns drove the protesters who gathered a few months later around meetings in progress at the International Monetary Fund and the World Bank.

The protesters also made known their fears that the emerging global market may ravage the environment. Many warned that corporations would site their plants in countries indifferent to protecting the environment. The result would be further damage to the already strained and polluted land and water resources of the developing world—resources needed to produce food in the battle against hunger. Also, these "runaway" plants could produce goods at lower cost than could businesses in countries that require them to take measures for the protection of the environment.

One need not agree with every protest registered in Seattle or the nation's capital to recognize, as President Bill Clinton did, that the demonstrators were entitled to be heard. Mr. Clinton has long been an advocate of an expanding international trading system. But he has also publicly conceded that such trade must be subject to certain protective regulations if it is not to damage the weak and the poor, undercut decent labor standards, and destroy the global environment. I am convinced that expanding trade, if guided by the public interest including fair labor and environmental standards, can result in greater production and better distribution of food—another potential building block for a world free from hunger.

Of equal concern to Third World farmers trying to succeed is the painful drop in economic assistance from more advanced countries. Severe cutbacks have been made in funds for agricultural research, irrigation, and extension services. There is no evidence yet that private capital will replace the reductions in foreign governmental assistance to these crucial farming enterprises. The cuts in such public investment are penny wise and pound foolish because they slow down the pace of rural development across the globe. That means less food and lower incomes for more than a billion people. Since this, in turn, means fewer customers who can afford to buy in the markets at home and abroad, everyone gets hurt.

It is perhaps worth noting that according to recent public opinion polls, the American public has an exaggerated notion of our foreign aid budget, estimating it to be about 15 percent of total federal spending. When asked what percentage of the budget should go to foreign aid, Americans suggested an average of 10 percent. Actually, less than 1 percent of the federal budget goes to foreign aid worldwide. The military's portion of the budget is 25 times larger. The United States devotes just 8/10 of 1 percent of its GNP to foreign aid, much less than Japan, Canada, Australia, and the countries of Europe. Also, much of American foreign aid is in the form of armaments to better-off countries rather than in the form of economic and technical assistance to the poor countries. Worldwide, the combined annual total of aid to the developing countries from the advanced countries is $50 billion—a decline of 16 percent in the last decade despite the larger population of today's world.

The other side of the coin is that if Third World countries are assisted more substantially in the development of their agriculture, water, and other resources, they will not only eat better, they will be better customers in international trade. If they are then given a fair break in international commerce, with counsel and instruction from their more experienced peers in Washington, New York, London, Paris, Berlin, Rome, and Tokyo, all of us will gain.

It is the political and moral responsibility of the international community to make certain that the new global economy does not widen the gap between the few nations that are wealthy and the vast majority that are poor. If this happens, the street demonstrations that rocked Seattle and the World Trade Organization will erupt elsewhere around the globe. Anyone who does any measure of traveling and speaking at home or abroad knows that when Q-&-A time begins, there will be tough, sometimes hostile, questions: "Isn't the World Trade Organization in the hip pocket of the conglomerates?" "Who will hire me when I am fifty if my company pulls up stakes and heads for South America and cheap labor?" "What do these big multinational corporations with headquarters in Tokyo or New York care about the environment in India, or Brazil, or Africa—or Wisconsin?"

Doubtless, these questions about the newly emerging global economy will proliferate. But if the answers are honest and the actions of the World Trade Organization and the nations it comprises are decent and just, then humanity will have taken another important stride toward freedom from hunger.

The continued liberalization of trade is inevitable; few would suggest going back to the bad old days of high tariffs and other restrictions that isolated national economies from each other. At the same time, allowing a totally unregulated global market to run amok would let hundreds of millions of people fall through the cracks. The liberalized global economy has created great wealth for a few and has provided new benefits and reduced hunger for many, but it has also increased hunger, insecurity, and misery for many others.

Food security has tended to increase in countries that open their economies to trade and international finance and has tended to decline in countries that have not. Economic growth rates have tended to rise as countries take steps to be more competitive, and, though the benefits have not generally been evenly shared within these countries, hunger has tended to decrease as a result. A key variable is how evenly the benefits of trade are distributed within a country. Until there are means of ensuring a more equitable distribution, poverty and hunger among the citizenry as a whole are not likely to be much reduced.

Free trade is not a sacred ritual proclaimed from on high. Without a moral underpinning and a reasonable measure of public regulation, trade can degenerate into hot commercial greed and the devil take the hindmost. In a brilliant discussion of these concerns while accepting the 2000 presidential nomination of the Green Party, Ralph Nader observed, "A society that has more justice needs less charity." Mr. Nader, whom I have long regarded as a national social conscience, added, "A just society is one that can better carry out the pursuit of happiness." It would be wonderful if the claims of justice could guide the emerging global economy.

Foreign direct investment has been very uneven: two-thirds of such investment in the developing world has gone to just eight countries, while more than half of all Third World countries, including virtually all of sub-Saharan Africa, have received little or none. Trade as a percentage of gross domestic product has declined in nearly half of Third World countries. East and Southeast Asia's export-oriented growth can be given a large degree of credit for the dramatic reduction in chronic hunger in that part of the world; the increase in hunger in Africa is related, in part, to the lack of such growth. Since China liberalized its economic trade policy in the late 1970s, poverty rates have plummeted by 60 percent and malnutrition has declined from 45 percent to 16 percent. Part of the credit can also be attributed to the move from large state-run farms to smaller family-run farms. It is important to note, however, that such economic benefits have been uneven and many people remain chronically undernourished—189 million in China alone. More crucially, over the past twenty years, more than 100 countries, with a population of more than 1.5 billion people, experienced a zero or negative per capita economic growth rate.

Only a small percentage of the more than $60 billion in food at retail prices imported yearly from the Third World to the industrialized world profits the farmers producing the food. Rather, the money goes largely to the traders, processors, shippers, and marketers. For example, of every dollar spent by American consumers for cantaloupes grown in El Salvador, the farmer gets less than a penny. Only 14 percent of what Americans pay for bananas grown in more prosperous Costa Rica goes to that country's people and government; the rest ends up in the hands of corporations and absentee foreign owners.

Another rather remarkable example of how unevenly the benefits of world trade are distributed: the American basketball star Michael Jordan annually makes more money for endorsing Nike shoes than the combined income of all 22,000 Indonesian women who make the shoes. It is not surprising that many of these women are hungry, despite their day-long toils at the assembly line. I do not object to Mr. Jordan getting rich. He has for years brought pleasure into our lives with his matchless athletic skill. What is objectionable is the near-starvation wages paid Indonesian working women.

Brazil, Bolivia, Thailand, and Chile, all of which have greatly expanded their agricultural exports over the past several decades, have failed to meet the food needs of their population. In some cases the situation has actually worsened. This is not surprising. Those who control the food production processes will naturally want to sell to those who can afford to buy at the best prices. Given that Third World traders can sell produce to industrialized nations at higher prices than their poor compatriots can afford, the market dictates that sellers should focus on exports. For example, although large numbers of Peruvians suffer from protein deficiencies, much of the fish caught in Peru's rich Pacific waters goes to North America for pet food. Why?

Because American pet owners can pay higher prices to feed their dogs and cats than Peruvian parents can pay to feed their children.

Again, the issue of land tenure becomes critical. Both the Central American nation of Costa Rica and the African nation of Kenya place considerable emphasis on export crops. The average Costa Rican, however, has benefited far more than the average Kenyan because most of Kenya's exports are grown on large plantations owned by a handful of wealthy families, while Costa Rica's export crops are grown by many small farmers. Other factors include Costa Rica's stronger tradition of democracy, good government, and demilitarization, as well as greater support for education, health care, land reform, and social insurance. As long as governments fail to address such issues as inequality and corruption, no trade policy can meet the food needs of their population.

If export earnings were shared throughout a country's population, food security for everyone would be enhanced. However, often a poor country's foreign exchange earnings are used to import luxury items for the wealthy instead of food for the hungry.

THE NORTH AMERICAN Free Trade Agreement (NAFTA) has provided new markets for some U.S. agricultural exporters, but has caused hardships for others. For example, tomato farmers in Florida have been run out of business by increased Mexican imports, not because the climate south of the border is necessarily better, but because Mexican tomatoes are cheaper. In anticipation of NAFTA's ratification, Green Giant closed its large Watsonville, California, plant and moved to Mexico to take advantage of cheaper labor. Comparative advantage seems less a matter of climate or other geographical endowments than of the ability of transnational corporations to move their operations to low-wage countries and to those whose governments offer conglomerates tax breaks and the relaxation of environmental regulations. When workers on Hawaiian pineapple plantations organized to achieve a living wage in the 1970s, Dole and Del Monte simply moved their operations to the Philippines, where labor unions were essentially banned and where land could be more easily purchased from poor, hard-pressed farmers.

Another problem is that the overall terms of trade in recent decades have been unfavorable to the poorer countries. Adjusted for inflation, export earnings for such raw materials as food crops, minerals, petroleum, coffee, tea, cocoa, and oilseeds have declined while prices for finished goods, such as high-tech products and services, machinery, transportation equipment, and farm equipment, have gone up. In other words, it now takes a lot more bags of coffee to buy a tractor.

UNFORTUNATELY, the globalization of the economy has made it easier for corporations to move to places with lower corporate taxes, lower wages, and less restrictive environmental standards.

Then there is the aforementioned incentive for developing nations to keep wages low so as to attract investment; this leads to situations like Indonesia's, where full-time assembly-line workers contracted by American corporations are often unable to afford basic foodstuffs for their

families. In many Third World countries, unions are sup-
pressed, working conditions are terrible, hours are long, and
wages often are insufficient to buy necessities. Even in the
United States, most poor people are working full-time, but
still find it difficult to feed, clothe, and house their families.
In South Dakota, I have seen the farm families whose toil
provides our food being forced to buy their own food with
food stamps. I have also seen American soldiers shopping
with food stamps to feed their families. Meanwhile, unemployment is at record levels in Europe and real wages are
declining throughout the industrialized world despite rela-
tive prosperity. The only way out of this "race to the bottom" is for nations to establish more humane minimal
standards. Much of the United States' prosperity can be attributed to the imposition of federal standards at the turn of
the last century. The federal laws made uniform the disparate state laws, which had provided little incentive to improve working conditions and promote overall economic
development. Professor Stephen Zunes of the University of
San Francisco has suggested that establishing global working
standards for a global economy would be a major step toward promoting justice for workers and for ending world
hunger. This might be something for the World Trade Organization member nations to consider.

Virtually all nations recognize that government-
administered economies are unworkable, that a market-
based system is the way to go, and that their economic
well-being is tied to being part of a globalized market system. But we must ensure that this dynamic system can meet
the food security needs of all. This will require establishing
some fair rules.

In summary, liberalized trade can increase economic
growth through greater efficiency and comparative advan-

tage. It tends to provide more choices and better quality for consumers at lower prices. It creates new jobs in poor countries. If the wage level were higher, it would be better not only for the workers in poor countries but also for their fellow workers in advanced countries such as the United States. Cheap labor abroad drives down wages in the developed countries. That is a major reason why American workers fear free trade and globalization. If, on the other hand, wages and environmental standards in the developing countries were raised to a fair level, liberalized trade would then create greater interdependence, growing trust, greater cooperation, and the reduction of misunderstandings. It is quite possible to recognize the great advantages of open trade and the market system without falling into the free-market fundamentalism that ignores the positive role governments and international standards can also play.

Early in my career, I remember, South Korea, Taiwan, and even Japan were suffering from serious shortages of food; large segments of their populations were hungry. These countries were able to turn themselves around, providing plenty of food for their own people and becoming net exporters of food by temporarily limiting food imports while embarking on an ambitious program of land redistribution and subsidies for domestic farmers and businesses. The idea was that by increasing the income and purchasing power of broad segments of society, they could develop an adequate consumer market to support their local economy, at which point they could drop many of their subsidies and tariffs and compete internationally. Indeed, the United States' first secretary of the treasury, Alexander Hamilton, set up similar protectionist measures to allow our infant national economy to compete with more powerful European economic powers. But such a strategy, which other countries might want to emulate, is no longer possible under the WTO's new rules. In the long run, however, the answer is not protectionism, but a liberalization flexible enough to meet varying national conditions. Freer trade should not be seen as a goal in and of itself, but as a vehicle for human betterment that takes into account the benefits as well as the costs, and modifies trade policies accordingly.

The continued emergence of a dynamic global economy, driven by trade and investment, seems to be a certainty. It can contribute significantly to ending human hunger, provided it has a human face sustained by a human heart. Free enterprise, yes, but free enterprise with a soul—even if that soul must sometimes come in the form of government regulation. It is sometimes argued that in the world of business and commercial trade, the only thing that matters is the bottom line. But let us hope that in the more enlightened precincts of commerce there is recognition of the wisdom propounded by Auguste Comte a century and a half ago: "Nothing at bottom is real except humanity."

As we have seen earlier in these pages, lifting our fellow humans out of hunger and enabling them to become constructive participants in the global economy is not only the morally right thing to do but will also add to our own prosperity and improve our hopes for peace and stability.

THERE ARE MANY commanding problems in the world, which probably all of us would like to see resolved. I suppose these would include militarism and war; racism, sexism, and other bigotry; environmental pollution; crime;

alcoholism and other drug addictions; poverty; the lack of family responsibility, including family planning; totalitarianism; illiteracy; and disease. It would be cause for universal rejoicing if we could somehow manage to resolve these problems in our time, by the year 2030.

But even confirmed optimists like me cannot honestly predict victory so soon over any of these long-standing curses of our civilization. I do believe deep in my soul, however, that we can and must end hunger in the world by the year 2030. I'm not referring to the temporary hunger that accompanies a war or civil conflict, or to hunger caused by catastrophes of nature that cannot be foreseen. Rather, I write of the chronic hunger of nearly 800 million people, who bear this affliction throughout their miserable, short existence on earth. There is no excuse for this kind of massive lifelong torture, ending only with an agonizing early death. Yet this is the fate that has been dictated from cradle to grave for one out of every seven human beings on our planet.

No war in all of history has ever killed so many humans and spread so much suffering and disease in any year as world hunger now does annually. So if we cannot resolve *all* of humanity's problems, let us resolve to end at least *one* by the year 2030—human hunger. If we fail to do this, we will stand condemned before the bar of history. In that case, shame on you and shame on me. If there is a scale of divine justice in the universe, we would deserve to choke on our food even as we listen to the cries of the starving.

I realize that as American ambassador to the UN agency responsible for much of what our nation does in the world of food and agriculture, I carry a heavier burden to discover salvation for the hungry than do my readers. But each of you can do something. Here are some possibilities:

(1) Make sure your church or synagogue or mosque has an overseas arm as well as a domestic outreach that is feeding the hungry. Give money to these efforts, or to such philanthropic agencies as CARE, Bread for the World, UNICEF, America's Second Harvest, the World Food Program, and the Food and Agriculture Organization of the UN.

(2) Quit complaining about the U.S. foreign aid budget, or at least that portion that feeds the hungry and helps farmers in the developing world produce better. Tell your representatives and senators to stop wasting money and lives shipping arms abroad and instead to do more to reduce human hunger. Foreign aid is a tiny part of our federal budget. Congress keeps cutting it. But if foreign aid is to be cut, let's reduce the destructive part, arms shipments, not the healing part, food to the hungry. The American Food for Peace program of the 1950s and 1960s, which I have studied intensely, did more to keep countries from slipping into Communism and despair than all the costly military hardware we shipped around the world during the Cold War, much of it to dictators who denied rather than advanced freedom. And as we have seen, feeding the hungry abroad enriched our farmers here at home.

It is popular in some quarters to pan our Department of State and its mission abroad. But let us not forget that the U.S. Foreign Service is widely respected as one of the best in the world. It is staffed by intensely patriotic Americans like ourselves. It keeps a close eye on developing trouble spots around the globe. It works hard to strengthen American economic security and political objectives abroad, including the development of markets for our agricultural and industrial goods.

(3) Become informed about the constructive work the United Nations does and, when possible, refute some of the

silly charges that are leveled at the UN by extremist groups. Let your friends and associates know about the work of such UN agencies as the Food and Agriculture Organization, the World Food Program, the International Fund for Agricultural Development, the UN Development Program, the World Health Organization, UNICEF, and other multilateral institutions, including the International Monetary Fund and the World Bank. Don't knock the UN. Recognize it as our best hope for international cooperation and peace, and a powerful tool in the battle against hunger, poverty, and disease.

(4) When you encounter an American farmer, rancher, or dairyman, tell him how much you appreciate the abundant food supply he makes available to us and to people around the world. Remind him of this truth: the American farmer is the most important person in the world. He keeps more people alive and healthy than any other individual. Ask him for his ideas on what could be done to end hunger abroad—and in America. If there were an international Farmers Corps to assist farmers abroad, would he or some member of his family be willing to serve in such a Corps? Would *you* be willing to serve for six months or a year in such an international effort to reduce hunger?

(5) If you should meet up with Bill Gates, Warren Buffet, Ted Turner (who has already generously given a billion dollars to the United Nations), or any other billionaire, ask him if he wouldn't like to ensure his place in heaven by investing a million or a billion in the triumph of humanity over the curse of hunger. He might say he is pursuing more important matters. If so, ask him to reduce his daily food intake to a crust of bread and a few spoonfuls of watery gruel for thirty days and then decide what is his most important interest and need.

Athletic coaches are adept at talking up the crucial importance of victory. The celebrated Washington Redskins coach George Allen once told his players at halftime of a bitterly fought football game: "When you guys get back out on that field, just remember you've got thirty minutes to live. Either you die, or you seize the victory."

To paraphrase this superheated coaching rhetoric, we have thirty years to bring hope and health and life to those now facing starvation around the globe. It is clearly within our power to win the victory in that time. That means we've got fifteen years until halftime, when 400 million of the world's 800 million hungry people should be eating adequately. We will then have fifteen more years in the second half to seize life over death for the remaining 400 million.

Doubtless there are sound ideas for ending world hunger other than the ones I have outlined. But I am convinced that the formula in the following nine-point summary can move the world to freedom from hunger by the year 2030.

1. A commitment by the President and Congress to end hunger in the United States during the first term of the president inaugurated in January 2001. This could be accomplished by a modest increase in the minimum wage and an equally modest enlargement of the food stamp program.

2. An assurance to American farmers, ranchers, and dairymen that if they continue to produce abundantly the Secretary of Agriculture will be authorized by Congress to purchase a reasonable portion of their surplus at a fair price for use in feeding the hungry at home and abroad.

3. The United Nations General Assembly should resolve that by January 1, 2030, there will be no

chronically hungry people in the world. The 1996 World Food Summit in Rome attended by nearly every country unanimously agreed to reduce by one-half the 800 million hungry people in the world by the year 2015. The UN agencies in Rome have adopted this objective. Now we need to make a firm commitment to reach the remaining 400 million hungry by 2030. That should be the most celebrated day in human history.

4. America should continue to take the lead in working through the United Nations and the private voluntary agencies toward a universal school lunch program, embracing every child in the world. In pledging $300 million of surplus farm produce to this proposal at the G-8 conference in Japan, President Clinton took a large first step. Senator Richard Lugar followed up with hearings on the concept before the Senate committee on Agriculture, Nutrition, and Forestry. Former senator Bob Dole and I led off the hearings with a joint bipartisan appearance.

5. The United States should take the lead within the United Nations and the private voluntary agencies in establishing a daily feeding program for pregnant and nursing mothers and their preschool children through age five. This program would be patterned after the highly successful American WIC program.

6. The United Nations agencies in Rome should establish carefully monitored grain reserves around the world to meet crisis situations, including natural disasters.

7. The UN Food and Agriculture agencies must ex-

pand and improve their efforts to assist Third World countries in strengthening their own production, processing, and distribution of food.

8. The United Nations should establish an international Farmers Corps patterned after the American Peace Corps but staffed largely by retired farmers and their wives to teach farm families in developing countries how to improve their operations. American farmers and their wives could play this role well.

9. The nations of the world should take full advantage of scientific agriculture, including the genetic modification of crops. Every scientific breakthrough in history has been greeted with controversy. Honest criticism should be given an honest answer. But there is little doubt that science can play an important and perhaps victorious role in the battle to achieve freedom from hunger.

As I have reached the end of this essay on world hunger, I have wondered how best to conclude it. There comes to mind a verse from the Hebrew Scriptures, by the ancient scribe Ecclesiastes: "To every thing there is a season, and a time to every purpose under the heaven" (Ecclesiastes 3:1).

I believe this is the season when all God's children the world over should launch a triumphant campaign to banish hunger from the earth. Can there be any higher "purpose under the heaven"?

ACKNOWLEDGMENTS

I AM GRATEFUL to the excellent research staffs of the three United Nations agencies in Rome that deal with the issues of food and agriculture worldwide. All of these agencies are engaged in expanding and safeguarding global food resources with special concern for the problem of world hunger.

I especially acknowledge my debt to Dr. Jacques Diouf of Senegal, the eminent Director General of the Food and Agriculture Organization, the oldest and largest of the UN agencies; Ms. Catherine Bertini, my brilliant fellow American, who heads the World Food Program; and Mr. Fauzi H. Al-Sultan, a highly esteemed banker who directs the International Fund for Agricultural Development. The research and advisory services of the U.S. Department of Agriculture headed by my much admired friend and former Kansas Congressman Secretary Dan Glickman; and the research services of the Department of State and the Agency for International Development have also been helpful. I owe a special debt to Professor Stephen Zunes of the University of San Francisco for his research assistance, especially with chapter 7. Congressman Jim McGovern of Massachusetts and Jeff Smith of the White House staff have supplied me with valuable additional materials. Professor Thomas Knock of the Southern Methodist University History Department, who has been working on a biography of me for several years, shared his research covering my long years of working on hunger issues both in the U.S. and abroad. His critical reading of this entire manuscript has improved it immeasurably. Professor Rainey

Acknowledgments

Duke of the English Department of Marshall University has again gone beyond friendship in searching my draft manuscript for literary and grammatical errors. My secretary, Pat Donovan, has typed and retyped, corrected and improved every page of this book, as she has my sometimes nearly illegible handwriting since I began public life as a young congressman in 1957. It's about time that I dedicate a book to this devoted friend and superb secretary of so many years.

I could in good conscience dedicate every book I write to my dear wife, Eleanor, as I have twice before. She is my most sensitive and perceptive critic. She never complains of an erratic writing agenda that sometimes has me writing through the night until after dawn.

Alice Mayhew, my editor at Simon & Schuster, was described to me by my friend Steve Ambrose as "the best in the business." I can now personally verify Steve's judgement. Her associate, Anja Schmidt, is first rate in her role—keeping an author on schedule, upgrading the text, and generally maintaining morale all around. I profited from a superb copy editor, Jolanta Benal, and excellent work on the interior book design by Ellen Sasahara and on the cover jacket by Jennifer Heisey. The publisher of Simon & Schuster, David Rosenthal, with whom I first worked when he was at Random House, is a treasured friend and literary advisor who has a way of inspiring me to do the best I can when I pick up my pen and begin to write. My agent, Esther Newburg, continues to represent my best interests in the publishing world.

My special assistant, Judy Edelhoff, and other members of my Mission staff in Rome, including staff director Laurie Tracy and overseas food and agriculture specialists Tim Lavelle and David Lambert, have cheerfully offered their valuable assistance.

INDEX

Index

Index

Index

Index

Index

obesity, 76
"Oil for Food" program, 60
Pakistan, 119, 138–39
Patton, Jim, 141
Payne, Harlan, 35
Peace Corps, 35, 46, 56, 68, 161
Peru, 28–29, 56, 66, 87, 150–51
pesticides, 36, 37, 41, 63
Pew Research Center for the People and the Press, 82
Philippines, 86, 138–39, 152
Podesta, John, 25–26
police force, international, 111–12
population growth, 11, 12, 38, 89, 117
Potrykus, Ingo, 41–42, 44
Program to End Hunger, A (Bread for the World Institute), 78–79
Public Law 480, 47, 49
Rabin, Itzhak, 114
Reagan, Ronald, 77
refugees, 59–60, 107, 110, 126, 130
religion, 17–18, 20, 45
  freedom of, 9, 108
rice, 36, 41–42, 63, 123
Rockefeller Foundation, 42
Ronald, W. R., 141
Roosevelt, Franklin D., 9, 22, 111
Rubin, Robert, 145
Rural Electric Cooperatives, 139–40
Russell, Richard, 30
Russia, 15, 24, 90, 108
Rwanda, 59–60, 94, 106
Sahel, famine in, 105, 106
Salish Indians, 127
Schlesinger, Arthur, Jr., 53–55
school breakfast programs, 75, 143
school lunch program, international, 25–34, 160
  locally produced food in, 31
  private voluntary agencies and, 27, 31, 32

WIC program compared with, 33–34
school lunch programs, 97, 143
  federal, 30, 56, 69–70, 74, 109
  in Food for Peace, 46, 56
Schorr, Dan, 73
Schumacher, E. F., 136
scientific agriculture, 11, 36–44, 161
Sen, Amartya, 88, 104
Sen, B. R., 57–58, 59
Senate, U.S., 49, 70, 112, 113–14
  Agriculture, Nutrition, and Forestry Committee, 71, 160
  Agriculture Committee, 26–27, 70
  Select Committee on Nutrition and Human Needs, 70–77
Senegal, 105
sexual abuse, 96–97
Shriver, Sargent, 46
Sierra Club, 43
Simon, Arthur, 78–79
Simon, Paul, 115–16
Small Is Beautiful (Schumacher), 136
Somalia, 103
Sorensen, Ted, 59
South Dakota, 19–23, 139
  farming in, 16, 19–21, 50, 140, 153
South Korea, 56, 122, 154
Soviet Union, 52–53, 73, 94
Special Supplemental Food Program for Women, Infants, and Children (WIC), 32–34, 61, 75, 160
Sperling, Gene, 25–26
Sri Lanka, 138–39
State Department, U.S., 51, 58, 59, 157
Stong, Ben, 70
Sudan, 103, 106
Sultan, Fauzi H., Al-, 66
summer feeding program, 74–75

170

Index

Index

ABOUT THE AUTHOR

GEORGE MCGOVERN was U.S. Senator from South Dakota from 1963 to 1981, and the Democratic candidate for President in 1972. He was the first director of the U.S. Food for Peace Program. Decorated with the Distinguished Flying Cross as a bomber pilot in World War II, he was awarded the Presidential Medal of Freedom in 2000. He holds a Ph.D. in history from Northwestern University. McGovern is now U.S. Ambassador to the UN Agencies for Food and Agriculture in Rome.